By Ishmael Reed

Essays
Writin' Is Fightin'
God Made Alaska for the Indians
Shrovetide in New Orleans

Novels
Reckless Eyeballing
The Terrible Twos
Flight to Canada
The Last Days of Louisiana Red
Mumbo Jumbo
Yellow Back Radio Broke Down
The Free Lance Pall Bearers

Poetry
Catechism of D Neoamerican Hoodoo Church
A Secretary to the Spirits
Chattanooga
Conjure

Plays
Mother Hubbard, *formerly* Hell Hath No Fury
The Ace Boons
Savage Wilds

Anthologies
Calafia
19 Necromancers from Now

Television Productions
Personal Problems
A Word in Edgewise

Writin' Is Fightin'

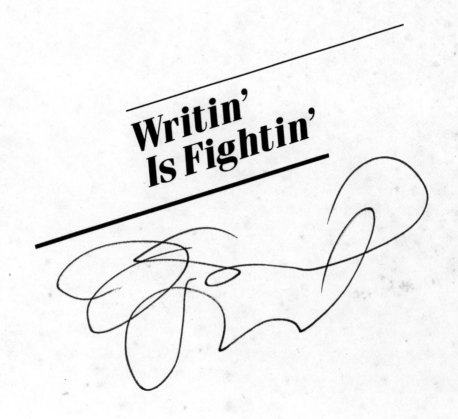

Ishmael Reed

Writin' Is Fightin'

Thirty-Seven Years of Boxing on Paper

Atheneum / *New York* / 1990

Collier Macmillan Canada   *Toronto*

Maxwell Macmillan International
New York   Oxford   Singapore   Sydney

"My Oakland, There Is a There There," Part I, first appeared in *California Magazine*, March 1983. Part II appeared under the title "At Ground Zero in Oakland" in the *San Francisco Examiner*, March 1988. "The Christmas Spirit" first appeared in the *Oakland Tribune*, December 1983. "America: The Multi-National Society" originally appeared in *San Francisco Focus*, December 1983. "300 Years of 1984" was delivered as a lecture as part of The George Orwell Series, Marin College, February 1984. "Hymietown Revisited" first appeared in *California Magazine*, October 1984. "Of One Blood, Two Men" originally appeared in the *New York Times*, 4 November 1984. "Dream Ticket" appeared under the title "Real Democrats Don't Eat Quiche" in *The Nation*, 6 April 1985. "How the Afrikaners Can Hold On" appeared under the title "Botha should take a tip on state-of-the-art apartheid from a real pro" in *The Tribune*, 23 August 1985. "Champion: Joe Louis, Black Hero in White America" first appeared in *The San Francisco Examiner*, January 1986. "In Opposition—Which State?" was delivered as a speech at the 48th International PEN Congress in New York City, 16 January 1986. "Hyped or Hip?" first appeared in *California Magazine*, March 1986. "Steven Spielberg Plays Howard Beach" originally appeared in *New York Amsterdam News*, January 1987. "August Wilson: The Dramatist as Bearer of Tradition" originally appeared in a somewhat different form in *Connoisseur*, March 1987. "Killer Illiteracy" first appeared in the *San Francisco Examiner*, November 1987. "America's Color Bind: The Modeling of Minorities" first appeared in the *San Francisco Examiner*, November 1987. "Soyinka Among the Monoculturalists" first appeared in *The New Theater Review*, a publication of the Lincoln Center Theater, Summer 1987.

Atheneum   Collier Macmillan Canada, Inc.
Macmillan Publishing Company   1200 Eglinton Avenue East, Suite 200
866 Third Avenue, New York, NY 10022   Don Mills, Ontario M3C 3N1

Library of Congress Cataloging-in-Publication Data
Reed, Ishmael, 1938-
    Writin' is fightin' : thirty-seven years of boxing on paper /
Ishmael Reed.
        p.   cm.
    ISBN 0-689-70734-7
    I. Title.
PS3568.E365W75   1990   90-46881   CIP
813'.54—dc20

Macmillan books are available at special discounts for bulk purchases for sales promotions, premiums, fund-raising, or educational use. For details, contact:

    Special Sales Director
    Macmillan Publishing Company
    866 Third Avenue
    New York, NY 10022

10 9 8 7 6 5 4 3 2 1

Printed in the United States of America

To the memory of John O. Killens
and James Baldwin and Allen Katzman,
"who fought the good fight"

A fighter fights, and a writer writes.

—*Chester Himes*

A black man is born with his guard up.

—*Paul Lofty*

Writin' is fightin'.

—*Muhammad Ali*

Don't bite your tongue about it.

—*Larry Holmes*

Contents

Boxing on Paper: Thirty-Seven Years Later

I n 1953, I was working in a drugstore on William Street in Buffalo, New York. As I left one evening to go home, a man pulled up to the curb and told me that he needed somebody to help him deliver newspapers. There were stacks of them in the backseat of his old brown beat-up Packard, which was just a shade darker than he was. His name was A. J. Smitherman, editor of *The Empire Star Weekly*, a Buffalo newspaper. How would you like to have this job every week? he asked after we'd taken copies of his newspaper to all of the newsstands on his route. I had been writing before then, and date my first commissioned work to 1952, when my mother asked me to write a birthday poem for one of her fellow employees at Satler's Department Store on Fillmore.

As a youngster, living in the projects, I also composed minisermons that I'd deliver during Sunday School from the pulpit at Saint Luke's Church, an old Afro-American Episcopal Zion church located on Eagle Street. But working at *The Empire Star* brought me into contact with articulate black people like Mary Crosby, Mr. Smitherman, and his son, Toussaint. Within a year, they even let me try my hand at writing columns, and I wrote jazz articles in what was to become a pungent writing style.

I drifted away from the *Star* in high school, having other things on my mind and needing more spending money than Mr. Smitherman was able to pay me. He was a relentless man who was barely able to bring out his newspaper every week. When he died, *The Buffalo Evening News* noted that he had to struggle against adversity. That's one of the things I remember about this gentle, intellectual editor and poet. His calm in the face of calamity.

As fate would have it, in 1960, after I'd dropped out of college and found myself, a father, living in the Talbert Mall Projects, attempting to support a family on forty dollars per week, I volunteered to do some work for the *Star*, which was then edited by Joe Walker, a dynamic young militant who was causing a stir in the city because of his fight against segregated schools and on behalf of Black Power. It was then that the lively style of my writing was put to the test. Fighting for a traffic light for my Talbert Mall neighbors (it's still there); debating the current mayor, James Griffith, on the subject of school segregation; defending black prostitutes who'd been brutalized by the police; and, at the same time, writing poetry and plays. The *Star* folded.

An Irish-American poet named David Sharpe liked a play of mine, and I traveled to New York with him one weekend. We spent most of the time at Chumley's, a restaurant located on Bedford Street in the Village. I was impressed. The book jackets of authors who'd drunk there, including Edna Saint Vincent Millay, lined the wall, and years later I felt that I'd arrived because mine went up. A screenwriter read my play standing at the bar (a play that was later lost in an abandoned car); he liked it.

After that, there was no keeping me from New York, and

a few weeks later, Dave and I went down on the Greyhound bus. I carried all of my belongings in a blue plastic bag I'd purchased for ten cents at the laundromat, and noticing my embarrassment, Dave carried it for me. It was 1962.

In New York, I joined the Umbra Workshop, to which Amiri Baraka credits the origin of the type of black aesthetic that so influenced the Black Arts Repertory School. It was in that workshop that I began to become acquainted with the techniques of the Afro-American literary style.

In 1965, I ran a newspaper in Newark, New Jersey, where I featured some of the same issues I'd covered in the *Star*, including a controversial piece on a welfare mother, which offended some blacks because she didn't sport the proper coiffure. It was during my tenure as editor of the *Advance* newspaper that I wrote an article about the police. Under heavy criticism, they'd invited members of the community to travel with them as a way of monitoring their activities. Representatives from the local civil rights organizations refused, but, in the interest of fair play, I accompanied them on their rounds one Saturday night, and because I commented that they had a tough job, I was called a right-winger by some black intellectuals.

I don't have a predictable, computerized approach to political and social issues in a society in which you're either for it or agin' it. Life is much more complex. And so for my early articles about black-on-black crime, I've been criticized by the left, and for my sympathy with some "left-wing" causes I've been criticized by the right, though from time to time I've noticed that there doesn't seem to be a dime's worth of difference between the zealotry of the left and that of the right.

I think that a certain amount of philosophical skepticism is necessary, and so regardless of the criticisms I receive from the left, the right, and the middle, I think it's important to maintain a prolific writing jab, as long as my literary legs hold up, because even during these bland and yuppie times, there are issues worth fighting about. Issues that require fresh points of view.

It was quite generous, I thought, for critic Mel Watkins to compare my writing style with that of Muhammad Ali's boxing style. My friend the late Richard Brautigan even saluted me after the publication of *Mumbo Jumbo*, my third novel, with the original front-page description of Jack Johnson's defeat of Jim Jeffries, printed by the *San Francisco Daily*, 4 July 1910. This, too, amounted to overpraise. If I had to compare my style with anyone's it would probably be with that of Larry Holmes. I don't mince my words. Nor do I pull any punches, and though I've delivered some low blows over the years, I'm becoming more accurate, and my punches are regularly landing above the waistline. I'm not a body snatcher like Mike McCallum, and I usually aim for the head.

A black boxer's career is the perfect metaphor for the career of a black male. Every day is like being in the gym, sparring with impersonal opponents as one faces the rudeness and hostility that a black male must confront in the United States, where he is the object of both fear and fascination. My difficulty in communicating this point of view used to really bewilder me, but over the years I've learned that it takes an extraordinary amount of effort to understand someone from a background different from your own, especially when your life doesn't really depend upon it. And so, during this period, when black males seem to be on somebody's endangered-species list,

I can understand why some readers and debating opponents might have problems appreciating where I'm coming from.

On a day in the 1940s, the story of the deportation of Jews to European concentration camps was carried in the back pages of a New York newspaper, while news of the weather made the front page. Apparently it was a hot day, and most people were concerned about getting to the beach. And so, during this period when American society begins to resemble those of feudal lore, where the income chasm between the rich and the poor is widening, when downtown developers build concrete and steel vanity monuments to themselves—driving out the writers, the artists, the poor, and leaving the neighborhoods to roaming drug-death squads (since all of the cops are guarding these downtown Brasilias)—it seems that most people are interested in getting to the beach and getting tanned so that they'll resemble the very people the media, the "educational" system, and the cultural leadership have taught them to despise (that's what I meant by blacks being objects of fear and fascination). The widespread adoption of such Afro-American forms as rock and roll can be viewed as a kind of cultural tanning.

And so as long as I can be a professional like Larry Holmes, that is, have the ability to know my way around my craft, I'll probably still be controversial. Arguing on behalf of the homeless, but at the same time defending Atlanta's middle-class leadership against what I considered to be unfair charges made by the great writer James Baldwin (no relation). And as I continue to practice this sometimes uncanny and taxing profession, I hope to become humbler.

I've had a good shot. It's almost a miracle for a black male writer to last as long as I have, and though some may regard me as a "token," I'm fully aware that, regardless of how some critics protect their fragile egos by pretending that black talent is rare, black talent is bountiful. I've read and heard a lot of manuscripts authored by the fellas over the years. The late Hoyt Fuller was right when he said that for one published Ishmael Reed, there are dozens of talented writers in the ghettos and elsewhere, who remain unpublished. And having lasted this long, I've been able to witness the sad demise of a lot of "tokens" who believed what their literary managers told them. Who believed that they were indeed unique and unusual.

Just think of all of the cocky boxers who got punched out by "nobodies" as they took on an unknown to warm up for their fight with the champion. In this business, spoilers are all over the place.

I was shocked to hear Secretary of State George Shultz acknowledge during the Iran-Contragate hearings what our cultural leadership, and "educational" defenders of Western civilization, fail to realize. That people are smart all over the world. I know that. I'm aware of the fellas, writing throughout the country in the back of beat-up trailers, in jails, on kitchen tables, at their busboy jobs, during the rest period on somebody's night shift, or in between term papers. All the guys burnt-out, busted, disillusioned, collecting their hundredth rejection slip, being discouraged by people who say they'll never be a champion, or even a contender. This book is for them. Writin' is Fightin'.

Oakland, California

My Oakland,
There Is a
There There

Part I

M y stepfather is an evolutionist. He worked for many years at the Chevrolet division of General Motors in Buffalo, a working-class auto and steel town in upstate New York, and was able to rise from relative poverty to the middle class. He believes that each succeeding generation of Afro-Americans will have it better than its predecessor. In 1979 I moved into the kind of neighborhood that he and my mother spent about a third of their lives trying to escape. According to the evolutionist integrationist ethic this was surely a step backward, since "success" was seen as being able to live in a neighborhood in which you were the only black and joined your neighbors in trying to keep out "them."

My neighborhood, bordered by Genoa, Market Street, and Forty-Eighth and Fifty-Fifth streets in North Oakland, is what the media refer to as a "predominantly black neighborhood." It's the kind of neighborhood I grew up in before leaving for New York City in 1962. My last New York residence was an apartment in a brownstone, next door to the building in which poet W. H. Auden lived. There were trees in the backyard, and I thought it was a swell neighborhood until I read in Robert Craft's biography of Stravinsky that when Stravinsky sent his chauffeur to pick up his friend Auden, the chauffeur would ask, "Are you sure Mr. Auden lives in this neighborhood?" By 1968 my wife and I were able to live six months of the year in New York and the other six in California. This came to an end when one of the people I sublet the apartment to abandoned it. He had fled to England to pursue a romance. He didn't pay the rent, and so we were evicted long-distance.

My first residence in California was an apartment on Santa Ynez Street, near Echo Park Lake in Los Angeles, where I lived for about six months in 1967. I was working on my second novel, and Carla Blank, my wife, a dancer, was teaching physical education at one of Eddie Rickenbacker's camps, located on an old movie set in the San Bernardino Mountains. Carla's employers were always offering me a cabin where they promised I could write without interruption. I never took them up on the offer, but for years I've wondered about what kind of reception I would have received had they discovered that I was black.

During my breaks from writing I would walk through the shopping areas near Santa Ynez, strolling by vending machines holding newspapers whose headlines screamed about riots in Detroit. On some weekends we'd visit novelist Robert Gover (*The One Hundred Dollar Misunderstanding*) and his friends in Malibu. I remember one of Gover's friends, a scriptwriter for the *Donna Reed Show*, looking me in the eye and telling me that if he were black he'd be "on a Detroit rooftop, sniping at cops," as he reclined, glass of scotch in hand, in a comfortable chair whose position gave him a good view of the rolling Pacific.

My Santa Ynez neighbors were whites from Alabama and Mississippi, and we got along fine. Most of them were elderly, left behind by white flight to the suburbs, and on weekends the street would be lined with cars belonging to relatives who were visiting. While living here I observed a uniquely Californian phenomenon. Retired men would leave their houses in the morning, enter their cars, and remain there for a good part of the day, snoozing, reading newspapers, or listening to the radio.

I didn't experience a single racial incident during my stay in this Los Angeles neighborhood of ex-southerners. Once, however, I had a strange encounter with the police. I was walking through a black working-class neighborhood on my way to the downtown Los Angeles library. Some cops drove up and rushed me. A crowd gathered. The cops snatched my briefcase and removed its contents: books and notebooks having to do with my research of voodoo. The crowd laughed when the cops said they thought I was carrying a purse.

In 1968 my wife and I moved to Berkeley, where we lived in one Bauhaus box after another until about 1971, when I received a three-book contract from Doubleday. Then we moved into the Berkeley Hills, where we lived in the downstairs apartment of a very grand-looking house on Bret Harte Way. There was a Zen garden with streams, waterfalls, and bridges outside, along with many varieties of flowers and plants. I didn't drive, and Carla was away at Mills College each day, earning a master's degree in dance. I stayed holed up in that apartment for two years, during which time I completed my third novel, *Mumbo Jumbo*.

During this period I became exposed to some of the racism I hadn't detected on Santa Ynez or in the Berkeley flats. As a black male working at home, I was regarded with suspicion. Neighbors would come over and warn me about a heroin salesman they said was burglarizing the neighborhood, all the while looking over my shoulder in an attempt to pry into what I was up to. Once, while I was eating breakfast, a policeman entered through the garden door, gun drawn. "What on earth is the problem, officer?" I asked. He said they'd got word that a homicide had been committed in my apartment, which I recognized as an old police tactic used to gain entry into somebody's house. Walking through the Berkeley Hills on Sundays, I was greeted by unfriendly stares and growling, snarling dogs. I remember one pest who always poked her head out of her window whenever I'd walk down Bret Harte Way. She was always hassling me about parking my car in front of her house. She resembled Miss Piggy. Though my landlord was a congenial intellectual, I came to think of this section of Berkeley as "Whitetown."

Around 1974, we found ourselves again in the Berkeley flats. We spent a couple of peaceful years on Edith Street, and then moved to Jayne Street, where we encountered another next-door family of nosy, middle-class progressives. I understand that much time at North Berkeley white neighborhood association meetings is taken up with discussion of and fascination with blacks who move through the neighborhoods, with special concern given those who tarry, or who wear dreadlocks. Since before the Civil War, vagrancy laws have been used as political weapons against blacks. Appropriately, there has been talk of making Havana—where I understand a woman can get turned in by her neighbors for having too many boyfriends over—Berkeley's sister city.

In 1976 our landlady announced that she was going to reoccupy the Jayne Street house. I facetiously told a friend that I wanted to move to the most right-wing neighborhood he could think of. He mentioned El Cerrito. There, he said, your next-door neighbor might even be a cop. We moved to El Cerrito. Instead of the patronizing nosiness blacks complain about in Berkeley, I found the opposite on Terrace Drive in El Cerrito. The people were cold, impersonal, remote. But the neighborhood was quiet, serene even—the view was Olympian, and our rented house was secluded by eucalyptus trees. The annoyances were minor. Occasionally a car would careen down Terrace Drive full of white teenagers, and one or two would shout, "Hey, nigger!" Sometimes as I walked down The Arlington toward Kensington Market, the curious would stare at me from their cars, and women I encountered would give me nervous, frightened looks. Once, as I was walking to the market to buy magazines, a white child was sitting directly in my path. We were the only two people on the street. Two or three cars actually stopped, and their drivers observed the scene through their rearview mirrors until they were assured I wasn't going to abduct the child.

At night the Kensington Market area was lit with a yellow light, especially eerie during a fog. I always thought that this section of Kensington would be a swell place to make a horror movie—the residents would make great extras—but whatever discomfort I felt about traveling through this area at 2 A.M. was mixed with the relief that I had just navigated safely through Albany, where the police seemed always to be lurking in the shadows, prepared to ensnare blacks, hippies, and others they didn't deem suitable for such a neighborhood.

In 1979 our landlord, a decent enough fellow in comparison to some of the others we had had (who made you understand why the Communists shoot the landlords first when they take over a country), announced he was going to sell the house on Terrace Drive. This was the third rented house to be sold out from under us. The asking price was way beyond our means, and so we started to search for another home, only to find that the ones within our price range were located in North Oakland, in a "predominantly black neighborhood." We finally found a huge Queen Anne Victorian, which seemed to be about a month away from the wrecker's ball if the termites and the precarious foundation didn't do it in first, but I decided that I had to have it. The oldest house on the block, it was built in 1906, the year the big earthquake hit Northern California but left Oakland unscathed because, according to Bret Harte, "there are some things even the earth can't swallow." If I was apprehensive about moving into this neighborhood—on television all-black neighborhoods resemble the commotion of the station house on *Hill Street Blues*—I was later to learn that our neighbors were just as apprehensive about us. Were we hippies? Did I have a job? Were we going to pay as much attention to maintaining our property as they did to theirs? Neglected, the dilapidated monstrosity I'd got myself into would blight the entire block.

While I was going to college I worked as an orderly in a psychiatric hospital, and I remember a case in which a man was signed into the institution after complaints from his neighbors that he mowed the lawn at four in the morning. My neighbors aren't that finicky, but they keep very busy pruning, gardening, and mowing their lawns. Novelist Toni Cade Bambara wrote of the spirit women in Atlanta who plant by moonlight and use conjure to reap gorgeous vegetables and flowers. A woman on this block grows roses the size of cantaloupes.

On New Year's Eve, famed landscape architect John Roberts accompanied me on my nightly walk, which takes me from Fifty-Third Street to Aileen, Shattuck, and back to Fifty-Third

Street. He was able to identify plants and trees that had been imported from Asia, Africa, the Middle East, and Australia. On Aileen Street he discovered a banana tree! And Arthur Monroe, a painter and art historian, traces the "Tabby" garden design—in which seashells and plates are mixed with lime, sand, and water to form decorative borders, found in this Oakland neighborhood and others—to the influence of Islamic slaves brought to the Gulf Coast.

I won over my neighbors, I think, after I triumphed over a dozen generations of pigeons that had been roosting in the crevices of this house for many years. It was a long and angry war, and my five-year-old constantly complained to her mother about Daddy's bad words about the birds. I used everything I could get my hands on, including chicken wire and mothballs, and I would have tried the clay owls if the only manufacturer hadn't gone out of business. I also learned never to underestimate the intelligence of pigeons. Just when you think you've got them whipped, you'll notice that they've regrouped on some strategic rooftop to prepare for another invasion. When the house was free of pigeons and their droppings, which had spread to the adjoining properties, the lady next door said, "Thank you."

Every New Year's Day since then our neighbors have invited us to join them and their fellow Louisianans for the traditional Afro-American good-luck meal called Hoppin' John. This year the menu included black-eyed peas, ham, corn bread, potato salad, chitterlings, greens, fried chicken, yams, head cheese, macaroni, rolls, sweet potato pie, and fruitcake. I got up that morning weighing 214 pounds and came home from the party weighing 220.

We've lived on Fifty-Third Street for three years now. Carla's dance and theater school, which she operates with her partner, Jody Roberts—Roberts and Blank Dance/Drama—is already five years old. I am working on my seventh novel and a television production of my play *Mother Hubbard*. The house has yet to be restored to its 1906 glory, but we're working on it.

I've grown accustomed to the common sights here—teenagers moving through the neighborhood carrying radios blasting music by Grandmaster Flash and Prince, men hovering over cars with tools and rags in hand, decked-out female church delegations visiting the sick. Unemployment up, one sees more men drinking from sacks as they walk through Market Street or gather in Helen McGregor Plaza on Shattuck and Fifty-Second Street, near a bench where mothers sit with their children waiting for buses. It may be because the bus stop is across the street from Children's Hospital (exhibiting a brand-new antihuman, postmodern wing), but there seem to be a lot of sick black children these days. The criminal courts and emergency rooms of Oakland hospitals, both medical and psychiatric, are also filled with blacks.

White men go from door to door trying to unload spoiled meat. Incredibly sleazy white contractors and hustlers try to entangle people into shady deals that sometimes lead to the loss of a home. Everybody knows of someone, usually a widow, who has been deceived into paying thousands of dollars more than the standard cost for, say, adding a room to a house. It sure ain't El Cerrito. In El Cerrito the representatives from the utilities were very courteous. If they realize they're speaking to someone in a black neighborhood, however, they become curt and sarcastic. I was trying to arrange for the gas company to come out to fix a stove when the woman from Pacific Gas and Electric gave me some snide lip. I told her, "Lady, if you think what you're going through is an inconvenience, you can imagine my inconvenience paying the bills every month." Even she had to laugh.

The clerks in the stores are also curt, regarding blacks the way the media regard them, as criminal suspects. Over in El Cerrito the cops were professional, respectful—in Oakland they swagger about like candidates for a rodeo. In El Cerrito and the Berkeley Hills you could take your time paying some bills, but in this black neighborhood if you miss paying a bill by one day, "reminders" printed in glaring and violent type-faces are sent to you, or you're threatened with discontinuance of this or that service. Los Angeles police victim Eulia Love, who was shot in the aftermath of an argument over an overdue gas bill, would still be alive if she had lived in El Cerrito or the Berkeley Hills.

I went to a bank a few weeks ago that advertised easy loans on television, only to be told that I would have to wait six months after opening an account to be eligible for a loan. I went home and called the same bank, this time putting on my Clark Kent voice, and was informed that I could come in and get the loan the same day. Other credit unions and banks, too, have different lending practices for black and white neighborhoods, but when I try to tell white intellectuals that blacks are prevented from developing industries because the banks find it easier to lend money to Communist countries than to American citizens, they call me paranoid. Sometimes when I know I'm going to be inconvenienced by merchants or creditors because of my Fifty-Third Street address, I give the address of my Berkeley studio instead. Others are not so fortunate.

Despite the inconveniences and antagonism from the outside world one has to endure for having a Fifty-Third Street address, life in this neighborhood is more pleasant than grim. Casually dressed, well-groomed elderly men gather at the intersections to look after the small children as they walk to and from school, or just to keep an eye on the neighborhood. My next-door neighbor keeps me in stitches with his informed commentary on any number of political comedies emanating from Washington and Sacramento. Once we were discussing pesticides, and the man who was repairing his porch told us that he had a great garden and didn't have to pay all that much attention to it. As for pesticides, he said, the bugs have to eat, too.

There are people on this block who still know the subsistence skills many Americans have forgotten. They can hunt and fish (and if you don't fish, there is a man who covers the neighborhood selling fresh fish and yelling "Fishman," recalling a period of ancient American commerce when you didn't have to pay the middleman). They are also loyal Americans—they vote, they pay taxes—but you don't find the extreme patriots here that you find in white neighborhoods. Although Christmas, Thanksgiving, New Year's, and Easter are celebrated with all get-out, I've never seen a flag flying on Memorial Day, or on any holiday that calls for the showing of the flag. Blacks express their loyalty in concrete ways. For example, you rarely see a foreign car in this neighborhood. And this Fifty-Third Street neighborhood, as well as black neighborhoods like it from coast to coast, will supply the male children who will bear the brunt of future jungle wars, just as they did in Vietnam.

We do our shopping on a strip called Temescal, which stretches from Forty-Sixth to Fifty-First streets. Temescal, according to Oakland librarian William Sturm, is an Aztec word for "hothouse," or "bathhouse." The word was borrowed from the Mexicans by the Spanish to describe similar hothouses, early saunas, built by the California Indians in what is now North Oakland. Some say the hothouses were used to sweat out demons; others claim the Indians used them for medicinal purposes. Most agree that after a period of time in the steam, the Indians would rush en masse into the streams that flowed through the area. One still runs underneath my backyard—I have to mow the grass there almost every other day.

Within these five blocks are the famous Italian restaurant Bertola's, "Since 1932"; Siam restaurant; La Belle Creole, a French-Caribbean restaurant; Asmara, an Ethiopian restaurant; and Ben's Hof Brau, where white and black senior citizens, dressed in the elegance of a former time, congregate to talk or to have an inexpensive though quality breakfast provided by Ben's hardworking and courteous staff.

The Hof Brau shares it space with Vern's market, where you can shop to the music of DeBarge. To the front of Vern's is the Temescal Delicatessen, where a young Korean man makes the best po'boy sandwiches north of Louisiana, and near the side entrance is Ed Fraga's Automotive. The owner is always advising his customers to avoid stress, and he says good-bye with a "God bless you." The rest of the strip is taken up by the Temescal Pharmacy, which has a resident health adviser and a small library of health literature; the Aikido Institute; an African bookstore; and the internationally known Genova Deli, to which people from the surrounding cities travel to shop. The strip also includes the Clausen House thrift shop, which sells used clothes and furniture.* Here you can

*Of all the establishments listed here, only the Siam restaurant, the Akido Institute, and the Genova deli remain.

buy novels by J. D. Salinger and John O'Hara for ten cents each.

Space that was recently occupied by the Buon Gusto Bakery is now for rent. Before the bakery left, an Italian lady who worked there introduced me to a crunchy, cookielike treat called "bones," which she said went well with Italian wine. The Buon Gusto had been a landmark since the 1940s, when, according to a guest at the New Year's Day Hoppin' John supper, North Oakland was populated by Italians and Portuguese. In those days a five-room house could be rented for forty-five dollars a month, she said.

The neighborhood is still in transition. The East Bay Negro Historical Society, which was located around the corner on Grove Street, included in its collection letters written by nineteenth-century macho man Jack London to his black nurse. They were signed, "Your little white pickaninny." It's been replaced by the New Israelite Delight restaurant, part of the Israelite Church, which also operates a day-care center. The restaurant offers homemade Louisiana gumbo and a breakfast that includes grits.

Unlike the other California neighborhoods I've lived in, I know most of the people on this block by name. They are friendly and cooperative, always offering to watch your house while you're away. The day after one of the few whites who lives on the block—a brilliant muckraking journalist and former student of mine—was robbed, neighbors gathered in front of his house to offer assistance.

In El Cerrito my neighbor was indeed a cop. He used pomade on his curly hair, sported a mustache, and there was a grayish tint in his brown eyes. He was a handsome man, with a smile like a movie star's. His was the only house on the block I entered during my three-year stay in that neighborhood, and that was one afternoon when we shared some brandy. I wanted to get to know him better. I didn't know he was dead until I saw people in black gathered on his doorstep.

I can't imagine that happening on Fifty-Third Street. In a time when dour thinkers view alienation and insensitivity toward the plight of others as characteristics of the modern condition, I think I'm lucky to live in a neighborhood where people look out for one another.

A human neighborhood.

Part II

*M*y Oakland, There Is a There There" was published in
1983. I returned to my house from Harvard on June 24, 1986,
to discover that crack operation had changed the neighborhood.
I became angry, disgusted, and frustrated. I tried to get my
feelings on paper as part of my stint as Writer-in-Residence for
the San Francisco Examiner. At the end of November, I was
optimistic that the downtown Oakland establishment would
put down what is amounting to a criminal uprising on the part
of the drug intermediaries. I'm writing this toward the end of
January, 1988; nothing has been done. The problem is getting
worse. I criticized James Baldwin for suggesting that the downtown Atlanta establishment only became interested in the child
murders occurring in working class neighborhoods when it began
to interfere with the tourist trade. Maybe I was wrong.

"I plan to investigate the possibility of placing Oakland under
a state of emergency."

The words, half-muttered by Lionel Wilson, the 75-year-
old mayor of Oakland, are such a shock that you react only
when you leave your interview with the mayor, the chief of

police, George T. Hart, and Henry Gardner, the city manager. He'd come a long way from November 2, when during a private dinner in the Claremont Hotel he said that the drug problem was confined to a few pockets in Oakland, and that the city manager was the only city official capable of doing something about it.

During our interviews with the city officials, there is much buck-passing. The city says it's the county's fault and the county passes the blame to the state and the federal government (which concentrates its aggression on Cuba and Nicaragua when the white garbage that's being exported into the United States by "friendly" countries like Colombia and Mexico is far deadlier than Marxist-Leninism). The courts put the criminals back on the streets because they have an overload, and the jails are full.

A frustrated and angry councilperson, Marge Gibson-Haskell, pleads with the citizens to cooperate with the police in identifying crack retailers, and the citizens say they don't trust the police, because if they, the citizens, can identify the crack dealers and their dope supermarkets, then why can't the police? One councilman says that there is so much cash in the crack industry, which according to some is America's leading commodity, that the police and the federal government might be in on the take. Another city official says that the federal government is prevented from cleaning up Oakland's crack problem because the Oakland police don't want outsiders on their turf.

The police, for their part, say that they can't go busting into a crack house without evidence of transactions, and even then they have to be mindful of the crackers' constitutional rights. Everybody says that they don't have enough money to do the job, but all agree that 18- to 24-year-old crackers are giving this grand, sexy, multicultural city—the most integrated in the country—a bad name.

And now, the mayor says that he is going to get a bulletproof vest and provide the kind of leadership that his critics say is long overdue; at the conclusion of this extraordinary November 9 interview in the mayor's office, Police Chief Hart commends the mayor for being a good shooter. The following Friday, you don't mention the state of emergency remark, but during a press conference where it's announced that Oakland's been declared a healthy city by the World Healthy Cities Organization—for some, an irony on par with that of one of Dracula's wives leading an aerobics class—you ask a question about another proposal the mayor made during the Monday interview.

In the midst of the usual happy talk about Oakland's image, the mayor answers unflinchingly that he plans to seek ways to outlaw Uzis, favorite weapon of the crackers. The downtown beautiful people present wince when you ask the question about the Uzis and as you exit, you extend your hand to one of them and he looks at it as though it were covered with snot. You've rained on his parade. This was supposed to be a day of celebration, and Uzis weren't supposed to be brought up. But you want to tell him and others like him in their pretty suits and fifty-dollar haircuts that if it weren't for the black working class like those domestics who brought segregated Montgomery, Alabama, to its knees, he and his other "new class" friends wouldn't be enjoying their prosperity. You want to tell him that it's the black working class—people who've put in time at stupid, dull jobs all of their lives, and suffered all manner of degradation so that their children might become achievers—that is bearing the brunt of the brutal crack fascists.

It is members of the black working class who are the victims of the drive-by shootings, burglaries, rapes, and assaults committed by the crack dealers and their clients. But you don't say it. You're so jubilant about the mayor's decision to bite the bullet, to finally offer some leadership against a problem that not only imperils Oakland but the survival of what the newspapers call Black America, that you forget the dozen chocolate chip cookies you bought on the way to the press conference, and when you return to ask the public information officer whether she's seen them she answers in a tone that signals she wasn't too pleased with your question about these semiautomatic weapons that are disrupting your sleep and the sleep of your neighbors.

She must have been surprised when a November 21 *San Francisco Chronicle* editorial congratulated the mayor on his frank answer to your question: "In his remarks, Mayor Wilson was realistic to the point of pain. He is to be commended for his willingness to speak honestly and to lead the fight on the drug-dealing plague." This from a newspaper that's often indulged in Oakland-bashing, the most unkind example of which appeared in a piece by columnist Jon Carroll entitled "Zany Oakland Hits Prime Time," in which Mayor Wilson was described as "the animal" who is "fifty percent Dacron and stuffed with cotton balls."

Finally, perhaps Oakland is prepared to face its high noon against the bad guys, even if it means a curfew aimed at the members of the 18- to 24-year-old age group that is causing the problems. Professor Troy Duster tells you that in view of the high unemployment rate among these black youths, it's amazing so few of them are involved in drug sales. According to U.S. Attorney Rudolph W. Giuliani of Manhattan, twenty-five other ethnic groups are in on the multibillion-dollar crack business. You know for a fact that some Asian Americans are among those who supply the North Oakland neighborhoods, but knowing this won't bring back four-year-old Kacherea Hollins, and United States track star Kerry A. Threets, both of whom were murdered by black terrorists, and it's these terrorists who are causing you and your neighbors so much misery.

As your wife, Carla, and your brother, Mike LeNoir, are discussing Oakland's number one health problem, the crack epidemic, Mike, who has a gift for the apt phrase, so evident in his sucessful health show on KCBS, contributes the metaphor you've been searching for. "It's like Chernobyl," he says. Your attitudes are based upon your distance from Ground Zero. Among those you interview, he and Councilman Wilson Riles, Jr., are the only ones who advocate legalization of drugs as a way of removing the criminal oppression now being experienced by Oaklanders, not only in the flats but in places like Montclair. This is a proposal that others find abhorrent. They don't live near Ground Zero, but there's drug dealing going on right across the street from Councilman Riles' house, and Michael LeNoir confronts Oakland's health problems firsthand, as a practicing physician. As you discuss the drug problem in Oakland with politicians, community leaders, men and women in the street, it does seem that the farther away you are from the situation, the more likely that your response is to be abstract and philosophical, and the more you're inclined to insist upon the constitutional rights of some of the most vicious enemies of black progress yet. Conversely, the closer you are to Ground Zero the more heat you're likely to feel, and to advocate primitive solutions such as vigilantism.

LaVonne Van, chairperson of a community group known

as ACORN, has her ear very close to the street, and she's heard talk of vigilantism. One man is always pulling his imaginary trigger finger when you ask him how he would deal effectively with the crackers. You can understand the position of both those at Ground Zero and those who are distant from it. In January 1986 there were signs that the situation, once limited to East Oakland, as far away from you as a Third World country, was moving closer to home—signs that you chose to ignore because you shared the lenient attitude of your generation toward drugs, and just before you left for Cambridge, Massachusetts, there was one of those police busts that you see on "Miami Vice" happening right under your nose. In Cambridge, you live the life of a Harvard Professor, residing in a condominium inside the Chester Kingsley mansion, a rambling Queen Anne number whose picture and history appear in a coffee-table book. In June, when you return to Ground Zero, you discover that what was once a tranquil North Oakland zone is occupied by a deadly army.

You discover that living in an area in which a crack den, smokehouse, or in the language of the police, problem house is in operation, is like living under military rule. Your neighborhood is invaded at all times of the day and night by armed men and women—death squads—who carry the kinds of weapons that are employed in small wars all over the world. People are trapped in their homes, intimidated by rival drug armies who on more than one occasion have caused the murder of innocent men, women, and children as they fight over the spoils. A policeman's comment to the press that only if you live in this kind of area are you likely to become a statistic, is not reassuring. The couriers, usually teenagers, ride bicycles; the suppliers drive Japanese pickup trucks or unlicensed Broncos; and the assassins ease by in BMWs, or in noisy, dilapidated hotrods with two people riding shotgun in the back and two up front. When their menacing sentries stand about on the lookout for cops, people don't dare come out of the house.

The retired people, single-parent families, and widows who used to take so much pride in the neighborhood stay indoors. The lawns are still kept up and the repairs done, but the mood is one of trepidation. You dread coming home because you never know when a car full of unsavory characters might be parked in front of your house, or a drug dealer's pit bull, "a dangerous weapon," might be running up and down the street unleashed and terrorizing the neighborhood children. The streets are quiet during the day, an improvement over the situation in June, but at night it sounds like troop movements. You think of the song, "The Freaks Come At Night." This must be how it is in Haiti under the Duvaliers, which is the kind of regime that comes to mind when you see the hoodlums milling about on your street. They have all of the charm of the Tonton Macoutes and wear the same kind of sunglasses. Robberies occur; within one month, four auto break-ins and four burglaries, as The Living Dead attempt to steal radios or anything that will finance their habit.

The patrolman who arrives after the second break-in of your car within the month of October says that the Oakland police can't cover all of the posts, and that stopping the cocaine epidemic is like stopping sand; Chief Hart says that his forces are "stretched thin," and that there should be more concentration on education; the people you see involved in the drug trade have been out of school for a long time. You hear this from most of the people you interview: the drug war is over and the bad guys have won. The chief of police cites all of the arrests that he's made, only to conclude that "the problem is getting worse. It's horrible." He tells this to the newspaper, a remark that is in sharp contrast to the conclusion of howdy-doody optimism reached by the Oakland Interagency Council On Drugs, November 1986: "there is a 'sense of containment' of the problem, and a perceived response from a previously protesting community of residents that progress is being made." On the other hand, Councilman Leo Brazile credits the agency with having successfully driven the street operations indoors where arrests are easier to make.

This crack stuff is cheap and highly addictive, and so some of the addicts come into your neighborhood three or four times during the night. They belong to the kind of armies that don't clean up after themselves, and so the morning after a night of cars arriving and departing every ten minutes or so, all of which seem to have bad engines and worse mufflers, your neighborhood sidewalks and streets are filled with the kind of dreck you find on the grounds of a drive-in theater the morning after a horror movie has played. The kind of people who seem to want to advertise the fact that they drink Wild Irish Rose and Night Train.

The horror movie metaphor is apt because the customers for this brain-scrambling stuff resemble cadavers as they wander in zombielike, some barefoot and wearing pajamas under overcoats. Some are obviously into prostitution to support their habit, and you read that in Chicago a woman sold her child for cocaine. In Oakland, another woman hid in the closet so her mother wouldn't share her profits. She was making one hundred dollars per day. So that her child wouldn't cry and her position be given away, she smothered the child to death.

A next-door neighbor said that he complained to the police

about "that house" but nothing was done. People say that they call the Oakland police and the police don't arrive, and when they do arrive they complain about how they're undermanned, and how budget cuts have harmed the force, and later you hear from Bill Lowe, a man who confronts drug dealers regularly with nonviolent techniques, that there have been no budget cuts.

The children are receiving an education about how low some adults can become. On the way to school they may have to step over some drug creep lying on their lawns, cracked into insensibility. You read about the effects of the drug operation on the psychological well-being of the children in Oakland. You really don't have to read; your daughter and the children on the block have nightmares about it. Drug dealers show up in their poetry.

No matter what you've done to maintain your house, your property value is reduced because who wants to buy a house in a neighborhood that has become a skid row, which is what can happen to a formerly decent neighborhood overnight, especially on the first and on the fifteenth when the welfare and Social Security checks are received.

This scene is spreading throughout Oakland. No matter what the people in the Junior League, the Lakeview Club, the ballet and symphony boosters may say about image, Oakland is in a state of war against drug fascists, and for the time being the drug fascists have gained the upper hand.

When you hear that the Oakland cocaine operation is a sort of take-out center for people in some of the more exclusive neighborhoods of Berkeley and Oakland, you wonder how many of the people in these exclusive neighborhoods have "Out of Nicaragua" bumper stickers on their Volvos, but are perfectly willing to tolerate drug fascists who prey upon the decent citizens of Oakland. You wonder how many agreed with a reporter for an alternative East Bay newspaper who just about drooled on his copy as he recorded the lurid activities of a heroin street dealer, making out as though this man were Robin Hood, or with another talented writer who made Felix Mitchell appear to be some sort of Mother Teresa—a man who headed an operation that took $50 million per year out of poor neighborhoods, enough to employ thousands of teen-agers during the summer. Anybody who praises a person who is trafficking in cocaine and heroin, when intravenous drug use may wipe out one-third of the black population—something that even the segregated regimes of the South and all of American racists combined haven't been able to accomplish—must be sick, and the admiration that some blacks have for these people must be the kind of twisted, perverted affection that a dog feels toward a master who sadistically tortures him.

What's hip about somebody who does errands for multi-national drug Caesars for the peanut end of the take? What's hip about somebody who puts blacks and Latinos in a position where they're spending billions of dollars on hard drugs, and in doing so financing the economies of Third World and Western countries; a sort of Marshall Plan whose bills are paid by the destitute? What's hip about somebody who doesn't have the sense to funnel his underground profits into community projects like the ethnic gangsters of the past, but sends money to the white suburbs because of his clownish, brazen lifestyle, which demands BMWs and gold-trimmed Rolls-Royces?

What's hip about drug dealers whose infamous activities attract bad media coverage and dissuade investors from coming into Oakland, therefore losing thousands of jobs for Oaklanders? George Williams tells you that some investors won't come into Oakland because they are afraid that their safety can't be guaranteed. What's so hip about crack merchants who, according to a theory proposed by Bill Lowe, chairperson of the North Oakland District Community Council, have joined with unscrupulous realtors to scare the black elderly out of town, and make room for regentrifiers? Books such as Jonathan Kwitny's *The Crimes of Patriots* claim that the contras are financing their despicable operations by dumping drugs into the poor neighborhoods of America, so what's hip about somebody who puts poor blacks and Latinos into a position where they're financing a foreign policy they might not approve of?

In Oakland, there are two governments, the legally elected representative government and the government of crackers who can make decisions about how your neighborhood should operate without calling public hearings, which is the way things are managed by their fellow fascist governments. As you think about all of this, you've worked yourself into a state of anger, and you feel like Paul Muni in *The Last Angry Man*. On July 1 you read that a 60-year-old man living in what is described as a quiet black neighborhood near the Berkeley border is caught in crossfire between some drug fascists and is paralyzed from the neck down.

When you attend a meeting of the Oakland Arts Council the next day, you say that this place is becoming like Beirut, and a couple of women who look like the Piedmont types who seem to rule over Oakland society and culture look at you as though you're crazy. They don't live at Ground Zero. You can imagine the same types in Munich, Germany, discussing a flower show, while Dachau was only an hour's drive from the city. When you read a few days later that the mayor says everything's fine, the developers' line, and that he can walk downtown anytime of day or night, you turn to your wife and say that the mayor ought to resign.

When novelist and librarian Kevin Starr calls to interview you for a piece about Oakland to be published in the October issue of *California Business*, you're angry as hell. You don't consider yourself to be left or right, or in the Ozzie and Harriet middle, though you visit the left more than you visit the other positions, but now you're beginning to sound like Judge Bork and you have to catch yourself. Shortly after the article is published you receive a call from Pauline Ford, an aide to Glenn Isaacson, vice president of Bramalea Pacific, the developer of City Center. She invites you to have dinner with him and the mayor.

She asks if you have seen the *California Business* article, in which you described the danger that the crackers are presenting to North Oakland, and where you responded to the mayor's claim that he can walk downtown with safety by saying that the neighborhood streets are narrower and meaner, while the boulevards downtown are wide. By the day of the dinner engagement you've heard some critical comments about the mayor from some of those you've interviewed. Not only does he lack the leadership ability necessary to solve the crack crisis, his critics say, but one person even suggests that he's in the pocket of the developers.

Councilman Leo Bazile says that if he were mayor he would use the office as a bully pulpit, and he would see to it that the city manager, who, because of the Oakland charter, runs the government, deals with the crisis effectively.

Wilson Riles, Jr., says that the mayor should visit every crack house in Oakland with a television crew, and by doing so expose the operations. You've also talked to former Berkeley Mayor Gus Newport, now a visiting fellow at a Boston college, who, though not critical of Mayor Wilson, agrees that you can't front an image of Oakland based upon some downtown paradise while a crime problem is attracting national attention. You've watched the mayor's combative style during the televised council meetings, but during the dinner, as you confront him with the criticisms of his style that you've heard, he listens patiently, without interrupting you.

So that those present don't believe that you're exaggerating, you bring two other residents of North Oakland who also live at Ground Zero, and it's the testimony of a mother who lives next to a crack house, not too far from your neighborhood, that stuns the gathering. You can tell that the mayor and Mrs. Isaacson are shaken. The waitress who serves the group has been nodding in agreement with the mother's testimony, and when you invite the waitress to contribute her comments, she says that she had just moved from East Oakland because the drug trafficking became intolerable. It's the mother's remarks that shock the mayor so much that he says later he didn't know the situation was that bad, and he quotes her during the press conference celebrating Oakland's health. He is to say of the dinner that he felt as though he had been eaten. The mood is somber when the dinner breaks up.

Glenn Isaacson, a man who seems genuinely concerned about the community in which he is doing business, invites you to visit the City Center development site. Kevin Starr calls you later in the evening to say that he hopes that the dinner has been productive. The mayor promises to arrange a meeting with you, himself, the chief of police, and the city manager. Though obviously upset by what he has heard at the dinner, he still insists that, by city charter, the drug crisis is the city manager's responsibility. On November 9, Monday morning, you feel that with Henry Gardner, the city manager, present, you're finally going to get some answers. You feel like Dorothy, about to meet the wizard.

During the meeting Police Chief Hart and the mayor recall the old days when you could tell a criminal to just get out of town. Though one high city official suggests to you that the first step in ending Oakland's crack problem is to ask for the retirement of Chief Hart, others credit the chief with having driven the major drug dealers out of business.

You finally question the city manager about his program for ending the drug terror, and he answers by describing his recent trip to England, and commenting on Toni Morrison's novel *Beloved*. It's when the mayor interrupts him that you realize that the mayor has already begun his crackdown on the crackers, an initiative that began the day after the dinner.

On the Saturday before your Monday morning meeting with Chief Hart, Mayor Wilson, and Henry Gardner, the city manager, you interviewed Bill Lowe and LaVonne Wilson. Bill Lowe, a resident of Oakland since 1924, had made the newspapers the day before with a comment that, he said, got him into trouble with some Oakland city officials. He told the *Chronicle* that Oakland was like Dodge City. This remark was his reaction to a shoot-out that was described under the head "Punks with Uzis Terrorize Oakland Flatlands." West Oakland's Acorn Apartments manager, Gerry Dickenson, was quoted as saying that the residents had gotten used to the gunfire. "It's not unusual for us to find forty-five or fifty bullet holes in apartments. Young punks just roam around with their Uzis, shooting into apartments." Maybe it's this weekend shoot-out or the testimony of the mother at the Claremont dinner, or both, but during this meeting the mayor agrees with Bill Lowe that posturing an unreal image of Oakland for the sake of attracting investors must take a backseat to dealing with the punks who are terrorizing the city.

Rev. Fred Shuttlesworth, in the acclaimed PBS series "Eyes on the Prize," says that you can't walk away from either physical or psychological oppression. And for those who believe that you can't do anything about crack because it's so prevalent, a comment that you heard often during your interviews, you think of the young martyrs whose lives we celebrate during these winter months. Suppose John F. Kennedy, Martin Luther King, Jr., Robert Kennedy—all of whom could have chosen lives of ease and comfort—had taken that attitude? You can't deal with a problem like racism because it's so prevalent. We'd still be in the back of the bus and eating at segregated lunch counters.

Crackers have to realize that people are not going to stand by as they destroy working-class America, and that if it comes to a choice between their survival and the people who form the incubator that produces black excellence, then most people will choose to side with the latter class without a moment's hesitation. Perhaps the mayor's new attitude will forestall what both Gus Newport and Troy Duster view as the ultimate tragedy: citizens taking the law into their own hands.

And if the mayor merely mentioned the state of emergency proposal as a trial balloon to see how much support he could muster, he might be interested to know that when you approached Supervisor John George about the idea on the Tuesday before Thanksgiving, he didn't reject the idea outright, but said he thought that the idea was intriguing—this from a man whose reputation as a "bleeding-heart liberal" ranks with that of Wilson Riles, Jr. An exasperated Riles tells you during your interview with him that we're just going to have to write some of these people off.

A couple of weeks before, you ran into Earl Caldwell, *Daily News* columnist, outside of a Lake Merritt grocery and he told you similar horror stories about the activities of crackers in New York. It's happening in Philadelphia, too. Earl said that these people are killing us. He said that we have to learn to fight black oppression as much as we fight white oppression: to demonstrate when a presidential candidate is murdered in Haiti, as well as against Botha's most recent antics. Both LaVonne Van and Bill Lowe laughed when you said, that morning in the Lake Merritt restaurant, that maybe the best way to solve Oakland's crisis would be to change all of the people directly involved in the crack terror to white. They agreed that there'd be demonstrations day and night and all of the local schools and universities would be shut down.

You finish your last essay as the *Examiner's* thirteenth Writer-in-Residence in an apartment the *Examiner* provides for the writers who are part of the series. From the window you can see the crowds visiting the bustling Fisherman's Wharf. According to an interview you conduct on the day before Thanksgiving with George Williams, the dynamic executive director of Oakland's Office of Economic Development and Employment, downtown Oakland will look like Fisherman's Wharf sooner than his critics think. He envisions a downtown Oakland that will receive 20,000 to 30,00 consumers per day. He has had to endure a different kind of heat during his eight years on the job, and has always managed to maintain his cool. He sees a future Oakland as being the hub of the entire East Bay. He rattles off the accomplishments of his office.

The Old Oakland project, developed by Richard and Glen Storek, will open next March. Thanks to Pacific Rim Travel, the occupancy of the Oakland Hyatt Regency is five percent above that of last year. A new $30 million, three hundred-room hotel will accommodate conventioneers who won't fit into the Hyatt City Square of the City Center project, and will include office space and retail shops. It will open early next year, and, according to Williams, the leasing is going well; it features an impressive rotunda that has already enhanced Oakland's skyline. EBMUD will soon construct a 250,000-square-foot office space project in Oakland's Chinatown. The sixteen Victorian homes that make up Preservation Park are close to finding a new developer. Construction on a new federal office building for downtown will begin in May.

Neighborhood projects include the Lincoln-Elmhurst development of housing and commercial facilities to be built on thirteen acres of land, and what promises to be a spectacular eight-acre complex at the Grove Street campus, which will include a supermarket of the caliber of Safeways and a housing development. At the moment Williams seems to be most excited about the successful wooing of Nordstrom's to Oakland. George Williams' vision of a Renaissance City competes with the drug dealers' creation of a war zone where nobody is safe. It remains to be seen which vision will prevail.

You spend your last day in the *Examiner's* apartment on Chestnut and Hyde putting final touches on one of the most depressing pieces you've written.

If you were a drinking man you'd fetch some George Dickel

whiskey, the concoction that kept you in a daze during your mid-twenties. Instead you walk down to the Exploratorium, and, coincidentally, the first exhibit shows that for you, there seems to be no escaping from Ground Zero. It reads: "Radioactivity spreads out just like light. The farther you move from a light source the dimmer it looks. The same applies to a radioactive sample. Particles stream from the source in all directions. When you move farther away, fewer particles hit you."

The Christmas Spirit

I f the United States were ever to be divided between schools of painting, the surrealists and their predecessors, the Mexican muralists could claim California. It is significant that the capital of America's voluptuous fantasies is located within this state. Unlike the ideal Christmas depicted on Hallmark cards—a Christmas of snow and sleigh bells—in California you celebrate Christmas among cacti and palm trees.

I remember an especially odd California Christmas during which a snowstorm occurred. So rare that my neighbors on Edith Street snapped pictures of it. California Christmases are vague, because in California there's no discernible change in the weather, causing Robert Louis Burgess to pen that immortal line, "seasons unseen as they pass."

If in popular song autumn is often a metaphor for middle age, winter has become a metaphor for these times. An apt image, though grim, is that of those innocent passengers of Korean Airlines Flight 007 at the bottom of the cold North Pacific—grieving relatives symbolically threw them winter clothes from a rented ship—treated like insects as they were caught in a squabble between the superpowers, "two scorpions in a bottle," victims of their angry poison. We watch entertainment-news horror stories about the arms race that might be extended into space, perhaps one day crowding out the North Star. It seems that a winter of the feeling is upon us and it won't go away, and because of El Niño (which some call "the Christmas child"), winters hang around longer than usual.

One can imagine ancient winter solstice men and women, thousands of years ago, praying for the winter to end and for the flowers to bloom (they liked flowers), and for the dead to go away—those who walked the long winter nights of Europe. Our reason for placing wreaths on our doors during Christmas is similar to the reason ancient people hung wolfsbane: to appease the dead and other creatures with supernatural powers. Sounds more like Halloween? The seasons are similar because during the Christmas season we are encouraged to wear the mask of goodwill, to party, and to buy presents, in what amounts to a hedonistic potlatch. Thousands of years after those early men and women, there's still no guarantee that spring will come. We get the Christmas blues, a pain that's hard to pinpoint, and we think that eating and drinking, and other "stress-related" activities, will make them leave.

Since 1979, I have been attempting to read the mystery of Christmas. So far, I have discovered that what many, including myself, dismiss as a frivolous event, celebrated in a country where *How to Flatten Your Stomach* is a best-seller, turns out to be a profound puzzle of beauty and depth. What is the message in the tangled and confusing story of the renegade and controversial Saint Nicholas, and what is the relationship between Nicholas and Black Peter, sometimes called his "helper" and in other versions his "master"? Why did Black Peter, introduced into Holland by the Spanish occupation, and the antecedent of the American Santa Claus, disappear from the American version, only to be replaced by the buffoonish, corpulent, department-store fool in the red suit (the invention of nineteenth-century political cartoonist Thomas Nast)?

Last year I attended the Saint Nicholas festivities in Holland, which marked the beginning of the Dutch Christmas. For hours, crowds milled about on several bridges until a barge, carrying Saint Nicholas—bishop's hat, robe, and staff—passed under the bridge and moved toward a dock. Starting at the ancient Saint Nicholas Church, Saint Nicholas, mounted on a splendid white horse, began a procession through Amsterdam, followed by Black Peter, who rode in a gray sports car from which he threw candy at the children who were yelling, "Pete! Pete!" It was a moving and entrancing scene, a ceremony I'd like to see repeated in Oakland or Berkeley, even though my Dutch friends dismissed it as commercial.

I came home to Oakland with Christmas artifacts, "evidence" that I will use in the remaining books of my Christmas trilogy, *The Terribles*. Among the collection is the Dutch edition of *Playboy* carrying the amazing cover of a female model with prominent breasts dressed as Black Peter, her face smeared with blackface. The statue of Nicholas, molded from white chocolate, disintegrated during the Royal Dutch flight.

Now, my house is full of Christmas objects that, in the beginning, were collected as research but have become an essential part of its ambience. My most prized possessions include a chocolate replica of Black Peter carrying a sack—it was also his job to go down the chimney, reward the nice, and punish the naughty—given to me by poet Jerome Rothenberg's son, Matthew, and a portrait depicting Saint Nicholas standing alongside two twin children in a tub. This was a gift from Professor Bob Thompson, who teaches a course called "The History of the New York Mambo" at Yale.

What is the message of Christmas? When one removes the distractions, the hard sell, the glitter, and the geegaw, there seem to be two: Faith is still a powerful force in human affairs, despite the jaded postmodernist disdain for sentimentality and for the maudlin; and each man, no matter how humble or obscure, can be touched by God. (Significantly, Christ was the first working-class god.) This is perhaps why Christmas has such wide appeal, celebrated in many countries of the world. Even the "atheistic" minority that composes Russia's ruling class wouldn't dare suppress Nicholas, more popular in Russia than Marx and the traditional patron saint of the working class.

America: The Multinational Society

At the annual Lower East Side Jewish Festival yesterday, a Chinese woman ate a pizza slice in front of Ty Thuan Duc's Vietnamese grocery store. Beside her a Spanish-speaking family patronized a cart with two signs: "Italian Ices" and "Kosher by Rabbi Alper." And after the pastrami ran out, everybody ate knishes.

(*New York Times*, 23 June 1983)

*O*n the day before Memorial Day, 1983, a poet called me to describe a city he had just visited. He said that one section included mosques, built by the Islamic people who dwelled there. Attending his reading, he said, were large numbers of Hispanic people, forty thousand of whom lived in the same city. He was not talking about a fabled city located in some mysterious region of the world. The city he'd visited was Detroit.

A few months before, as I was leaving Houston, Texas, I heard it announced on the radio that Texas's largest minority was Mexican American, and though a foundation recently issued a report critical of bilingual education, the taped voice used to guide the passengers on the air trams connecting terminals in Dallas Airport is in both Spanish and English. If the trend continues, a day will come when it will be difficult to travel through some sections of the country without hearing commands in both English and Spanish; after all, for some western states, Spanish was the first written language and the Spanish style lives on in the western way of life.

Shortly after my Texas trip, I sat in an auditorium located on the campus of the University of Wisconsin at Milwaukee as a Yale professor—whose original work on the influence of African cultures upon those of the Americas has led to his ostracism from some monocultural intellectual circles—walked up and down the aisle, like an old-time southern evangelist, dancing and drumming the top of the lectern, illustrating his points before some serious Afro-American intellectuals and artists who cheered and applauded his performance and his mastery of information. The professor was "white." After his lecture, he joined a group of Milwaukeeans in a conversation. All of the participants spoke Yoruban, though only the professor had ever traveled to Africa.

One of the artists told me that his paintings, which included African and Afro-American mythological symbols and imagery, were hanging in the local McDonald's restaurant. The next day I went to McDonald's and snapped pictures of smiling youngsters eating hamburgers below paintings that could grace the walls of any of the country's leading museums. The manager of the local McDonald's said, "I don't know what you boys are doing, but I like it," as he commissioned the local painters to exhibit in his restaurant.

Such blurring of cultural styles occurs in everyday life in the United States to a greater extent than anyone can imagine and is probably more prevalent than the sensational conflict between people of different backgrounds that is played up and often encouraged by the media. The result is what the Yale professor, Robert Thompson, referred to as a cultural bouillabaisse, yet members of the nation's present educational and cultural Elect still cling to the notion that the United States belongs to some vaguely defined entity they refer to as "Western civilization," by which they mean, presumably, a civilization created by the people of Europe, as if Europe can be viewed in monolithic terms. Is Beethoven's Ninth Symphony, which includes Turkish marches, a part of Western civilization, or the late nineteenth- and twentieth-century French paintings, whose creators were influenced by Japanese art? And what of the cubists, through whom the influence of African art changed modern painting, or the surrealists, who were so impressed with the art of the Pacific Northwest Indians that, in their map of North America, Alaska dwarfs the lower forty-eight in size?

Are the Russians, who are often criticized for their adoption of "Western" ways by Tsarist dissidents in exile, members of Western civilization? And what of the millions of Europeans who have black African and Asian ancestry, black Africans having occupied several countries for hundreds of years? Are these "Europeans" members of Western civilization, or the Hungarians, who originated across the Urals in a place called Greater Hungary, or the Irish, who came from the Iberian Peninsula?

Even the notion that North America is part of Western civilization because our "system of government" is derived from Europe is being challenged by Native American historians who say that the founding fathers, Benjamin Franklin especially, were actually influenced by the system of government that had been adopted by the Iroquois hundreds of years prior to the arrival of large numbers of Europeans.

Western civilization, then, becomes another confusing category like Third World, or Judeo-Christian culture, as man attempts to impose his small-screen view of political and cultural reality upon a complex world. Our most publicized novelist recently said that Western civilization was the greatest achievement of mankind, an attitude that flourishes on the street level as scribbles in public restrooms: "White Power," "Niggers and Spics Suck," or "Hitler was a prophet," the latter being the most telling, for wasn't Adolph Hitler the archetypal monoculturalist who, in his pigheaded arrogance, believed that one way and one blood was so pure that it had to be protected from alien strains at all costs? Where did such an attitude, which has caused so much misery and depression in our national life, which has tainted even our noblest achievements, begin? An attitude that caused the incarceration of Japanese-American citizens during World War II, the persecution of Chicanos and Chinese Americans, the near-extermination of the Indians, and the murder and lynchings of thousands of Afro-Americans.

Virtuous, hardworking, pious, even though they occasionally would wander off after some fancy clothes, or rendezvous in the woods with the town prostitute, the Puritans are idealized in our schoolbooks as "a hardy band" of no-nonsense patriarchs whose discipline razed the forest and brought order to the New World (a term that annoys Native American historians). Industrious, responsible, it was their "Yankee ingenuity" and practicality that created the work ethic. They were simple folk who produced a number of good poets, and they set the tone for the American writing style, of lean and spare lines, long before Hemingway. They worshiped in churches whose colors blended in with the New England snow, churches with simple structures and ornate lecterns.

The Puritans were a daring lot, but they had a mean streak. They hated the theater and banned Christmas. They punished people in a cruel and inhuman manner. They killed children who disobeyed their parents. When they came in contact with those whom they considered heathens or aliens, they behaved in such a bizarre and irrational manner that this chapter in the American history comes down to us as a late-movie horror film. They exterminated the Indians, who taught them how to survive in a world unknown to them, and their encounter with the calypso culture of Barbados resulted in what the tourist guide in Salem's Witches' House refers to as the Witchcraft Hysteria.

The Puritan legacy of hard work and meticulous accounting led to the establishment of a great industrial society; it is no wonder that the American industrial revolution began in Lowell, Massachusetts, but there was the other side, the strange and paranoid attitudes toward those different from the Elect.

The cultural attitudes of that early Elect continue to be voiced in everyday life in the United States: the president of a distinguished university, writing a letter to the *Times*, belittling the study of African civilizations; the television network that promoted its show on the Vatican art with the boast that this art represented "the finest achievements of the human spirit." A modern up-tempo state of complex rhythms that depends upon contacts with an international community can no longer behave as if it dwelled in a "Zion Wilderness" surrounded by beasts and pagans.

When I heard a schoolteacher warn the other night about

the invasion of the American educational system by foreign curriculums, I wanted to yell at the television set, "Lady, they're already here." It has already begun because the world is here. The world has been arriving at these shores for at least ten thousand years from Europe, Africa, and Asia. In the late nineteenth and early twentieth centuries, large numbers of Europeans arrived, adding their cultures to those of the European, African, and Asian settlers who were already here, and recently millions have been entering the country from South America and the Caribbean, making Yale Professor Bob Thompson's bouillabaisse richer and thicker.

One of our most visionary politicians said that he envisioned a time when the United States could become the brain of the world, by which he meant the repository of all of the latest advanced information systems. I thought of that remark when an enterprising poet friend of mine called to say that he had just sold a poem to a computer magazine and that the editors were delighted to get it because they didn't carry fiction or poetry. Is that the kind of world we desire? A humdrum homogenous world of all brains but no heart, no fiction, no poetry; a world of robots with human attendants bereft of imagination, of culture? Or does North America deserve a more exciting destiny? To become a place where the cultures of the world crisscross. This is possible because the United States is unique in the world: The world is here.

300 Years
of 1984

I was tempted to title my remarks about George Orwell "White Man's Utopia Is a Black Man's Dystopia," after Muslim Minister Louis Farrakhan's 1960s calypso hit, "The White Man's Heaven Is a Black Man's Hell," until it occurred to me that, although any journalist or critic can refer to me as black, my very use of the word "white" marks me as a racist. This points to a double standard regarding what ethnic and racial designations mean, and the personal motives of those who use them. In fact, one could argue that the very words "white" and "black"—terms created by ancient American slave masters in order to create a cheap labor supply—are polarizing, given the conflict between these concepts in English, a conflict that has been frequently documented.

A sign of how enormously the media influence cultural and political trends in American life can be found in Theodore Bernstein's account of how the newspapers chose the term "black" over "Afro-American," because the word "black" was easier to set in headlines. I have noticed over the years that critics have often referred to me as a "black" without revealing their own ethnic backgrounds. This matter has become one of the themes of a new novel entitled *Reckless Eyeballing*, which means that people can define me and even profit from interpreting what they call "the black experience" (think of all of the millions non-Afro-American producers, artists, and writers have made from interpreting "Afro-American culture" through novels, film, music, and television—so much so that it's debatable whether the culture is "ethnic").

Afro-American culture, it often seems, is every American-European's third heritage. Even my writing students who are not Afro-American do not hesitate to create Afro-American characters and to employ what they feel are Afro-American speech patterns and styles, yet when Samm-Art Williams, an Afro-American playwright, wrote about the Nazi holocaust from the point of view of its victims, or when novelist Willard Motley created characters with an Italian background, their attempts were viewed as out of line.

Richard Wright's *Savage Holiday*, a novel which includes major "white" characters, has been viewed as a curiosity. However, no one blinks an eye when Francis Ford Coppola produces a film based upon Afro-American culture, *The Cotton Club*, or when John Sayles produces a miserable racist film that he calls a "black" horror movie; indeed, critics often write about nonwhite cultures as though their only reason for existence is to influence American-European artists. Fifteen thousand years of Native American poetry is important because it inspired what the Native Americans call "white shamans," like Walt Whitman. Rock and roll is important because it inspired Mick Jagger. We are spear-carriers in this great epic entitled "Western civilization," or "Judeo-Christian" culture, a phrase which makes you wonder why the Christians have given the Jews such a hard time for hundreds of years. Our attempts to write about other major cultures is considered a case of "Reckless Eyeballing." What you lookin' at? This is none of your business.

Some may view my attempt to comment on George Orwell's 1984 as a case of Reckless Eyeballing. Looking at something that doesn't concern me.

After viewing the science fiction movie 2001, many Afro-American patrons commented about the absence of Afro-Americans in Arthur C. Clarke's and Stanley Kubrick's future world. In Ernest Callenbach's novel Ectopia, about a future quiche-and-sushi California paradise, the Afro-Americans are shunted away into pogroms. It's not that there is no room for groups other than privileged European males in the future; the problem for talents like Clarke and Callenbach is that they are writing from a limited point of view. They live in a world blind to the existence of what they refer to as "minority men," and to women. It's their viewpoint that's ethnic, if the word "ethnic" has come to mean narrow-minded. They cannot face the facts of a world of diverse cultures and people. 1984 is the monocultural nightmare. Writing from a restricted point of view, Orwell failed to see that for millions of his contemporaries, 1984 had already arrived. In the United States, Afro-Americans have been witnessing 1984 for over three hundred years. One can conclude that it is better to suffer from Reckless Eyeballing than to suffer from the disease that afflicted Winston Smith and his group of elitist intellectuals who provide the Big Brothers of the world with their information and attitudes. The disease of cultural astigmatism.

George Orwell's vision of a grim totalitarian dictatorship that he predicted would be in place by the year 1984 has provided Communists and anti-Communists with an opportunity to indulge in their usual name-calling and finger-pointing. Anti-Communist ideologues claim that the party and political order of *1984* resembles the regime that controls the Soviet Union. Orwell's Eurasia could very well be the Soviet Union. People of the West refer to the Russians as "Mongolian hordes" when they get mad at them, as when the South Korean Flight 007 jet was shot down over Soviet territory, Ms. Jeane Kirkpatrick, in a private speech before the Heritage Foundation, attributed the existence of a "totalitarian" system to Russia's history of "Oriental despotism," indicating that the political feud between the Soviet Union and the United States might be more racial than ideological.

Further evidence that Orwell had the Soviet Union in mind might be garnered from the fact that *1984*'s secret doctrine was based upon a slogan used to popularize one of Stalin's five-year plans. Certainly Goldstein, the party's archenemy, bears a relationship to Stalin's archenemy, Trotsky, in physical description, and like Trotsky, Goldstein wrote a book about a revolution being betrayed. Yet the author points out in several passages during the course of the book that the techniques used by the Soviet Communist party and the German Nazi party are quite crude in comparison with those exercised by the Party in *1984*. "The German Nazis and the Russian Communists come very close to us in their methods but they never had the courage to recognize their own motives. They pretended, perhaps they even believed, that they had seized power unwillingly and for a limited time, and that just around the corner there lay a paradise where human beings would be free and equal. We are not like that," Winston's interrogator, O'Brien, says at one point. The fact that the Soviet Union has banned the book *1984* has been viewed as proof that their government sees the book as being critical of their system. For the Soviet Union, Orwell was a "Socialist renegade," and in December of 1984 a Latvian dissident was arrested by Soviet authorities and sentenced to seven years hard labor for having a copy of the book in his possession. On January 26, 1983, a Soviet publication called *The Literary Gazette* went so far as to charge that it was really the United States Orwell had in mind when he invented the totalitarian government of Oceania, and pointed to parallels between life in that made-up country and life in the United States, which like Oceania lies in the middle of two oceans. The article argued that Newspeak, doublethink, and the Thought Police can be found in American life. One might reply that a government that bases its principles upon the often wordy and obscure jargon of Karl Marx has a lot of nerve accusing a rival government of using Newspeak and doublethink. Both governments are guilty of that. One could even say that those neoconservative critics who use the book *1984* as a way of condemning Soviet society are also guilty of Newspeak and doublethink. (I have a hard time deciding whether it's neoconservatism they're pushing, or whether they use the term as a cover for neo-Nazism.)

Speculation concerning the author's intentions and the accuracy of his prophecies has become a blue-chip industry. I'm amazed that the people who gave us Monopoly haven't invented a game called 1984. United Technologies placed an ad in *Harper's* magazine that claimed that Orwell's vision of a sinister technology used to keep its citizens in line was wrong. "Technology has not enslaved us, but freed us," the ad announced, which ought to reassure those who are worried about the military uses of space or chemical and nuclear technology. Even the contemporary manufacturers of telescreens and speakwriters got into the act. Apple Computer Company portrayed Big Brother as the IBM Company, while Apple's MacIntosh computer presumably represents the proles who would one day overtake Big Brother and overthrow Big Brother and his party. (If Orwell had a chance to write *1984* from the vantage point of 1984 instead of 1948 perhaps he would have seen the class of hackers instead of the class of proles as a threat to Big Brother's rule.)

Whose side was Orwell on? He has been called a capitalist, but most of his comments about capitalism are ironic and descriptive and do not constitute an endorsement of the capitalist system over the socialist system. The description of capitalist attitudes toward the proles given by the old men Winston encounters in the pub during his search for clues about the past seem pretty accurate to me.

"They owned everything that there was to own. They lived in great gorgeous houses with thirty servants, they rode about in motor cars and four-horse carriages, they drank champagne, they wore top hats . . . they and a few lawyers and priests and so forth who lived on them—were the lords of the earth. Everything existed for their benefit. You—the ordinary people, the workers—were their slaves. They could do what they liked with you. They could ship you off to Canada like cattle."

And it does in no way serve as a vehicle for the author's praise of capitalism. Orwell's cynicism, which comes through in his biting descriptions of characters, who are often mangled by the author, indicates a "plague on both your houses" attitude toward capitalism and communism as economic systems. His misanthropic inclinations might be traced to the tuberculosis he suffered while writing the book and may also account for the book's apocalyptic vision.

Even though the author's praise for the proles—eighty-three percent of Oceania is prole, and they are permitted a freedom the Party members are denied and even sass the Thought Police—his description of the proles is reminiscent of those employed by American literature's archsnob Henry James in his story "Brooksmith." They don't speak English correctly. Their tastes are bad; their children are savages; they smell of "hideous . . . sour beer"; they're the only members of the population permitted to enjoy sex, for the Party believes that "only proles and animals are free." The Party doesn't even deem it necessary to install telescreens in their homes. (In fact, one could say that the proles in *1984* are better off than the contemporary proles. The *1984* proles are encouraged to reproduce while there is evidence that many of today's proletariat women—Native American, black, and poor—have been sterilized without their permission.) While Winston Smith shares the attitude of *1984*'s author George Orwell regarding the proles, that "If there was hope, it must lie in the proles, because only there, in those swarming disregarded masses . . . could the force to destroy the Party ever be generated," Smith's ambivalent view of the proletariat reminds one of the attraction-revulsion ideas concerning the working class held by a group of intellectuals, sanctioned by the American media as the United States' official intelligentsia, the New York intellectuals, or the Family. Those who abandoned Marxism and left-wing politics for the religion of aesthetic traditionalism, or neoconservatism, after being disillusioned by Joseph Stalin and hounded by Joe McCarthy.

Their attitudes are mercilessly satirized in Mary McCarthy's superb book *The Oasis*. Although they spend a lot of time denying their power, they set the trends of not only American literature but Afro-American literature as well, a literature they view as part of a separate tradition, treating it as such in their journals, in which all "black" writers are lumped together.

Many of these ex-socialists have made their career out of criticizing popular culture, the Third World, the grass roots, populism, the underclass, and the rest of the labels they apply to the rest of us. Like them, Winston Smith, whose favorite word seems to be "rubbish," wanders about searching for a lost tradition and commenting on the decline of good tastes. The book includes endless dawdling about the lack of "good books," chocolate, cigarettes, wine, whiskey (Party intellectuals drink Victory gin; the masses, beer), and good English (though the author of 1984 constantly confuses "one another" with "each other"). Winston Smith longs for antiques: china, glass, brass candlesticks, all suggesting a nostalgia for what the Party condemns as ownlife, and what the Marxists referred to as bourgeois individualism. If the world of 1984 is one of dystopia, then utopia for Winston Smith would be a long dinner party on the Upper West Side of New York that would include much prattle concerning abstract things, or a gourmet tour of Berkeley.

As a novel, 1984 contains flaws that creative writing students are always warned to avoid. The author bullies both the readers and his characters with lengthy amateur psychoanalysis (another New York intellectual pastime) of their motives, which puts him in the position of a literary Big Brother submitting the characters in his fiction, for whom he has little regard, to thought control. His repetitious and often confusing and contradictory descriptions of the political system of his fictional world interrupt the story line, his narrative often deteriorates into cant and polemics, and his often meanspirited prejudices seem odd and puzzling. Some of his scenes are embarrassingly and unintentionally funny, as when he has the lovers Winston and Julia meet in a church that has been A-bombed thirty years before. His love scenes contain descriptions that one associates with pulp writing: "She twisted herself round and pressed her bosom against him. He could feel her breasts, ripe yet firm, through her overalls. Her body seemed to be pouring some of its youth and vigor into his." For a book touted for its glimpse into a future sinister technology, most of the technology—the telescreen and the speakwrite rockets—is based upon primitive prototypes that were available in Orwell's time.

However, at least Orwell had the daring to make a guess and take a chance in a form—the novel—whose practitioners often take the easy way out, writing books with conventional plots and predictable characterizations that indolent critics demand be "well-rounded"; books that lack the fresh imagery one expects of the poet. One can say that Orwell's *1984* is at least interesting and different. He deserves a high mark for imagination and it is a tribute to him that many of his predictions about the state of things in the year 1984 have come true. Two political cyclops that one might call Oceania and Eurasia are at loggerheads and a world, scared to death, looks on helplessly. Giant and mindless bureaucracies inspect the actions of citizens as though they were Orwell's "beetles under a microscope." (It's not the crude torture devices or the horrors of Room 101 that ultimately get Winston Smith to confess, but the endless questioning by bureaucrats: "Their real weapon was the merciless questioning that went on and on hour after hour, tripping him up, laying traps for him at every step of lies and self-contradiction, until he began weeping as much from shame as from nervous fatigue." Anyone who's ever had a driver's test knows the feeling.)

How accurate was George Orwell's projection concerning the surveillance of contemporary citizens by a totalitarian government? A survey conducted on September 1, 1983 of 1256 people, paid for by the Southern New England Telephone Company, found that the percentage of Americans who are "very concerned" about threats to personal privacy had increased from thirty-one percent in 1978 to forty-eight percent in 1983. Those who believed that their privacy was being invaded cited collection and sharing of data about them by the IRS, FBI, census bureau, phone companies, banks, loan companies, credit bureaus, and other agents of the private and government sectors as a cause for alarm. Modern citizens not only have to fear surveillance conducted by their government, but surveillance by enemies of the government as well.

According to *The Berkeley Review*, 2 February 1984, "competent technical sources" indicated that "the Soviet Consulate in San Francisco has the resources and capability of intercepting important microwave telephone transmissions in the area."

Microwave interception is just one of the toys used by governments and the private sector to keep tabs on citizens. Also available, according to *Security World*, the trade journal of the industrial security field, are "infra-ultrasonic detectors sensitive to noise or motion, electric eyes which activate cameras and silent alarms in stockrooms and other 'high security areas,' infrared detection systems, motion detectors, bugging devices, debugging devices, paper shredders, and virtually everything else the imagination can conceive."

Orwell was correct, and his prediction concerning the extent of surveillance to which contemporary citizens are subjected by government and the private sector falls on the conservative side.

Moreover, the physical torture inflicted upon dissenters and ownlifers continues. It sometimes seems that torturing other people still ranks as one of mankind's chief pleasures and pastimes. In April 1984, Amnesty International described the methods of torture that are used in at least one-third of the world's nations, including the Soviet Union and the United States. They include pain-inducing drugs given in "psychiatric clinics," "beatings, electrical and acid torture, the spraying of tear gas into the faces of prison inmates." In Iran's Evin prison, the report noted, "small children are forced to watch their mothers being tortured."

Some people didn't have to wait until 1984 for this kind of relentless torture and surveillance to happen to them. For Afro-Americans, it could be argued that every year they've spent in this country since they arrived in chains to perform forced labor has been 1984. For the first three hundred years, those who considered them to be property kept tabs on their every action, or relegated this task to a class of Overseers and Patrollers, Big Brother's human surveillance equipment of the time.

As Julia and Winston's love affair was broken up by the authorities, many slave men and women were forced to go their separate ways or betray each other for fear of torture, and now, because of welfare eligibility requirements in some states, they must live apart or starve. The knock at the door at night has always meant for Afro-Americans the possibility that white men have arrived to take you somewhere to torture you or to lynch you: the Klan, the Nazi party, the FBI, the state, county, and local police, as well as any number of vigilante groups.

Behavior modification involving drugs and other technologies has been regularly practiced on Afro-American men and women, and quack scientists have been permitted to use them as guinea pigs in infamous and Nazi-styled experiments such as the Tuskegee syphilis experiments. When Nixon's adviser, Arnold Hutschnecker, proposed to test children for antisocial behavior, he had Afro-American children in mind.

There are other parallels between the terrors experienced by the Party members in 1984 and those Afro-Americans have experienced throughout their history in the United States.

In 1984, literacy is discouraged by the state. When Winston Smith is arrested, his diary is used as evidence against him. During the period of slavery, a slave who read or wrote could be maimed or killed, and even in modern times an Afro-American writer's words have been used against him, as both Langston Hughes and W. E. B. Du Bois discovered when they testified before the contemporary version of the Thought Police, the House Un-American Activities Committee. Even though European-Americans were humiliated and psychologically tortured by the same forces, Afro-Americans always seem to get the worst of it. No white man has been spied upon the way Marcus Garvey, Malcolm X, or Martin Luther King, Jr., who was encouraged by the FBI to commit suicide, were spied upon.

But we found out about the hideous surveillance of those men through the Freedom of Information Act, and this is the reason why I feel that it is Winston Smith's class of elitist intellectuals and monoculturalists (called the "Town Set" by populists of the 1880s) who are more likely to bring about the kind of world that George Orwell envisioned than any American government, for no matter what totalitarian tendencies it might have, no matter how many Huston Plans a government might be tempted to try, sooner or later an administration, no matter how abhorrent its policies, will leave office, and there's always the possibility that whatever excesses it may have condoned will be exposed.

But there seems to be no way to remove the party intellectuals whose ideas control the media, and by media I mean any industry involved in communications: television, radio, newspapers, the universities, and culture; in fact, it has sometimes been the government that has made an effort to moderate the resistance of this class to multiculturalism in American society, and to the participation of women and minority men in the communications industry. It has been government reports that have exposed the domination of the media by men of the same class and interests. It is members of this class—sometimes referred to as "the brightest and the best"—who counsel politicians, and they who train politicians how to think.

Winston Smith's attitudes toward women and minority men are typical of the attitudes held by this class. The women who appear in *1984* are either stupid or childlike. It is they who are the most susceptible to the teachings of Big Brother. They are zaftig slumgoddesses with mountainous, earth-mother bodies—the salt of the earth—or they are fallen women like Julia, who admits to having slept with a number of men, among them hypocritical Party members. That's all right, Winston Smith says. I don't like pure things anyway. In *1984*, a Third World man has a walk-on. He is described as "the little yellow-faced servant . . . carrying a tray with a decanter and glasses." The other nonwhites are off somewhere in Asia or Africa, scene of Orwell's Armageddon.

For "the brightest and the best," the Party intellectuals, the cultures of women and minority men have been vaporized and flushed down the memory hole. Winston Smith's job is that of doctoring history, of vaporizing and distorting things. Winston Smith accuses his interrogators of embracing a primitive solipsistic philosophy, "the belief that nothing exists outside of your own mind," but cannot see his own solipsistic attitudes and those of his Brotherhood.

What went wrong in Lebanon? How did we lose Vietnam? Where are we? What's going on? the politicians ask as they lurch from disaster to disaster. For the Party intellectuals, nothing exists outside of their monocultural view of things. They don't explain to the Big Brothers they serve that with the shrinkage of the world that has occurred because of modern communications technology, lazy and inarticulate responses —brute force—no longer work.

The ambassador to the United Nations is the author of a number of crude remarks expressing a contempt for internationalism and what she and her staff refer to as the "Third World." She caught the eye of the administration after her articles appeared in *Commentary* magazine, a hangout for the right-wing branch of the New York intellectuals. These monoculturalists discourage any contact with other cultures abroad and at home. The Party discourages the learning of foreign languages, reminiscent of the contemporary antibilingual education campaign here at home (when the American hostages were seized, nobody in the American Embassy could speak to the Iranians in their language). They desire that everybody be ignorant like them, yet the mass media refer to them as intellectuals when one Paul Metcalf, or one Wendy Rose, or one Toni Cade Bambara is worth more than the whole crowd.

Instead of attempting to communicate with other cultures at home and abroad, members of the Family like Midge Decter and Nathan Glazer attempt to engage them in endless competition over who is going to be their most beloved "minority." Nathan Glazer wants to know why Afro-Americans haven't made it while the Indians and the Hispanics have. Nathan Glazer wants to take a peek at our chromosomes to see if that's the reason why Afro-Americans haven't made it. The New York intellectual is bent upon "making it." To be in a position to influence public policy. To be invited to dinner by the White House and be told that the president liked your arguments opposing affirmative action. Making it.

Their counterparts in the television, movie, and newspaper industries are constantly subjecting women and minority men to "Hate Week," exciting the population with inflammatory disinformation smears against them, the way the media in 1984 stir up hatred against the Eurasians and the East Asians. We're criminals and brutes to them; they like us to be like Mr. T, a playful though menacing brute who is in a constant state of belligerency. Savages. They even hate mild-mannered people like Michael Jackson and Larry Holmes and Mayor Bradley, excoriating them and their achievements in hateful vitriolic column after column. It is this malice and cultural astigmatism that will eventually lead to the downfall of the Party, Winston Smith's people. They can't see us but we can see them. They don't know us but—as multicultural writers—we know them at their worst and at their best. To them, we are ethnics; to them, we are the proles, a name I'm sure they would apply to writers like Leslie Silko, Lorna Dee Cervantes, Andy Hope,

Sister Goodwin, Nash Candelaria, and Simon Ortiz, American aristocrats whose ancestors were among the first families of North America.

Their almost-religious clinging to monocultural values and their insistence upon intellectual obedience to what they and Winston Smith refer to as "tradition" has contributed to the United States' warped perception of the world and of cultures at home. They have given the American eye a bad dose of cultural astigmatism. They are the true Thought Police, and what's the difference between the current fundamentalists' drive for an Establishment Church and their desire to impose their values upon the rest of us in what was meant to be a pluralistic society?

Orwell's *1984* is rich in resonance and lends itself to many interpretations, the essence of modern art. It is poetic, and packed with sharp and insightful proverbs, but at the same time prolix and speckled with bad writing. But it is still a great book and a great work of art in the same sense that *Uncle Tom's Cabin* and *Native Son* are great works of art, because they inspired, and because they sprang from, the soul, which is the source of all great art. Handel said that when he wrote the *Messiah* God had visited him, and with *1984* the spirit visited George Orwell, and the result is this handwriting on the wall, this warning to future generations of what happens when truth and art disappear from a society.

Will Orwell's idealistic hope ever come true? Will the proles overthrow Big Brother and his intellectuals, the Party? That game is still being played, but it's quite possible that this generation will witness the final outcome of this old battle. As the middle class vanishes all over the world, this weary, beat-up-on class that has served as a buffer between the rich and the poor, the world will be divided between Big Brother and the proles, and if the proles do overthrow Big Brother and his overclass intellectuals, maybe they will have the tolerance that was never shown toward their cultures, maybe they will have the good sense to spare the Party its greatest nightmare, that the cultural annihilation they practiced toward others will not be aimed at them, and that the abuse and the torture they meted out to others will not be meted out to them.

It is significant that George Orwell, who served British imperialism in Burma, casts Winston Smith's chief interrogator as the Irishman O'Brien.

Hymietown Revisited

Jesse Jackson's private description of Jewish Americans as "Hymies" lacked good judgment, but those who argued that a white presidential candidate would have been driven from public life for making a similar statement—an assertion made by Jackson critics during the 1984 presidential primaries—are mistaken. Similar statements have been made by presidents, presidential candidates, vice presidents, prominent political supporters of candidates for high office, and some of Jackson's press critics.

While governor of California, Ronald Reagan *publicly* referred to Afro-American men as "strapping bucks"; ridiculed homosexuals (their place, he said, was in the "Department of Parks and Recreation"); implied that African leaders were cannibals ("when they have a man for lunch, they *really* have him for lunch"); and made a remark during the 1980 campaign that I would nominate for the tasteless jokes Hall of Fame:

"How do you tell the Polish one at a cockfight?"

"He's the one with the duck."

"How do you tell the Italian?"

"He bets on the duck."

"How do you know the Mafia is there?"

"The duck wins."

He wasn't required to grovel for this gaffe, which slurred two ethnic groups, and the episode was quickly forgotten.

His vice president, George Bush, coined the ignominious phrase "voodoo [sic] economics"; "voodoo" being a derogatory name for Vodun, an Americanized African religion whose followers, in this hemisphere, number in the millions. Imagine the uproar that would have occurred had a politician used the term "Christian economics" as a synonym for the ridiculous!

The Nixon tapes revealed that the former president disparaged both Jews and Afro-Americans while in office. He told his daughter to avoid the New York art world because it was dominated by Jews.

Nixon referred to Afro-Americans as "jungle bunnies" and considered them inferior to European Americans.

Neither Ronald Reagan nor Richard Nixon were driven from public life; to the contrary, the *San Francisco Chronicle*, which has carried comments by some of Jackson's most relentless critics—William Safire, Abe Mellinkoff (relentless), George Will, and others—published an editorial on August 5, 1984, titled "Nixon's Comeback."

Among Jackson's critics in the press, James Reston and William Buckley, Jr. published awkward comments about Irish Americans and Chinese Americans. Reston characterized Irish people as warlike in remarks about President Reagan's "getting his Irish up" (*New York Times*, 15 April 1984). The same Reston referred to Jesse Jackson as "cheeky." Chinese Americans were characterized as "Chinks" on the cover of William Buckley, Jr.'s *National Review* (4 May 1984). I would be surprised if the Republican party repudiated one whose written works helped to shape Mr. Reagan's political ideas.

William K. Coors recently stereotyped Africans as backward. One could argue that the bond between Coors and the Republican administration is stronger than that between Jesse Jackson and Louis Farrakhan during the presidential primaries, since it was the Adolph Coors Company that provided seed money to the Heritage Foundation, the ultraright-wing think tank that influences the administration's policies.

As for Jackson's "Hymietown" remark, Jackson traced it to small-town experience. Where Jackson lived in Chicago, "Hymietown" was where you went for discounts when you couldn't afford to buy a suit in the downtown department stores, he explained. He said that he meant no offense by the remark.

When it comes to religious and ethnic tolerance, the United States often behaves like an overgrown small town with its Hymietown, Chinktown, Dagotown, Micktown, Japtown, Niggertown, and Spictown, while interests the nineteenth-century populists described as the "Town Set" preside over it all and often appear to be egging the mobs on against one another and rewarding with "Angloness" those "white" ethnic groups which stave off the "nonwhite" hordes.

American cultural institutions seem so bent on preserving the values of "Western civilization," the mythical "Whitetown," that we learn about one another's cultures the same way we learn about sex: in the streets.

Three hundred and twenty-five scholars, journalists, teachers, and governmental and cultural "leaders" were invited by William J. Bennett, chairman of the National Endowment for the Humanities, to name books that every student "might reasonably be expected to have studied before he or she graduates from high school." Of the thirty most frequently named, eleven were written by Americans, five of which were published in this century. Only one American female writer made the list. No Afro-American, Hispanic, Asian-American, or Native American literature was included.

If the people who chose the list of thirty books are intellectual and cultural "leaders," then it is no wonder that the way different groups communicate with one another in the United States often takes on the appearance of a rumble.

I don't believe that Jackson, Reagan, Hart—who came in for criticism from Arab Americans for his use of terms like "Arab blackmail"—or any of the others whose errors I've cited committed them out of any meanness or desire to hurt the groups that were offended by their remarks. However, the fact that the others escaped the kind of chastisement that Jackson received indicates that even when we try to be noble by condemning bigoted remarks, we behave in a bigoted manner.

Of One Blood,
Two Men*

*W*hile the Puritans sometimes executed their children in order to teach obedience, we today—with somewhat the same mistaken approach to correction—send criminals to prison, only to teach them to become better criminals. As Robert Wideman—the younger brother of the Rhodes Scholar and award-winning novelist John Edgar Wideman—says in *Brothers and Keepers*, "By the time a dude gets out of here, most likely he's a stone criminal, or thinks he is. They got professors and Ph.D.'s in crime giving crime lessons in here. . . . You learn how to go for the big time."

Brothers and Keepers is John Edgar Wideman's gripping account of the events, social pressures, and individual psychological responses that led his brother Robert to prison for murder and him to a middle-class life as a professor of English at the University of Wyoming in Laramie. By combining his own literary skill with the candor and vitality of his brother's street style, Mr. Wideman gives added power and dimension to this book about the contrary values and goals of two brothers. It is a rare triumph in its use of diverse linguistic styles; the

*A review of *Brothers and Keepers*, by John Edgar Wideman, Holt, Rinehart and Winston, 1984

result is a book that has the impact of reading Claude Brown's powerful *Manchild in the Promised Land* and James Weldon Johnson's elegant *The Autobiography of an Ex-Colored Man* in alternating paragraphs.

John Edgar Wideman and Robert Wideman, who is ten years John's junior, were born to the same Pittsburgh family, but that's about all they have in common. John has become the author of six novels (including *Sent For You Yesterday*, which won the PEN/Faulkner Award in 1983) and is a college professor with an attractive family and a Volvo station wagon. Robert Wideman is serving a life sentence at Western Penitentiary in Pittsburgh. Much of the book deals with how the two men arrived at such different destinies, or as the line from the Sly Stone song, "A Family Affair," quoted in the book says: "One child grows up to be somebody/who just loves to learn/And the other child grows up to be/Somebody who just loves to burn."

John Wideman's thoughts about the question are more complex. "People and events take shape not in orderly, chronological sequence," he writes, "but in relation to other forces and events, tangled skeins of necessity and interdependence and chance that after all could have produced only one result: what is. The intertwining strands of DNA that determine a creature's genetic predispositions might serve as a model for this complexity, but the double helix, bristling with myriad possibilities, is not mysterious enough." The Widemans' dedicated mother, Betty, is more to the point in explaining Robert's "wildness": "That's how he's been since the day the Good Lord put him on His earth."

Pittsburgh's seedy Homewood district provided Robert's destructive characteristics with the perfect feeding ground. He wanted to be a "player," a "rebel," to "party hearty." He mocked the "straight-square" goals of his brothers and sisters who received good grades and did right. "No way Ima be like the rest of them niggers scuffling . . . to get by. Scuffling . . . till the day they die and the shame is they ain't even getting by. They crawling. They stepped on." He would have none of this. He wanted to be "stone Hollywood . . . stone sharp. . . . We the show people. The glamour people. Come on the set with the finest car, the finest woman, the finest vines . . . What else a dude gon do. . . . You make something out of nothing."

Desiring to make something out of nothing, Robert and his friends pool their money and buy heroin for resale to addicts, but instead of becoming the ghetto Superflies of their ambitions, they have the luck of the Three Stooges in a farcical but deadly tragedy. The heroin they buy goes bad. Robert gets sick from it. He and his friends lose their jobs. As a way of raising cash to buy more heroin, they try to run a variation of the Murphy game on a fence, only this time, instead of using nonexistent prostitutes as the bait, they promise the fence, who is white, nonexistent hot television sets.

The scam works if you take the fence's money and run, leaving him in the lurch, stranded in a hostile neighborhood. Instead, the scam backfires and in the resulting confusion the fleeing fence is shot in the shoulder after one of Wideman's companions mistakenly believes that the fence is harboring a weapon. The shoulder wound turns out to be fatal, and Robert is informed the next day by the partner who actually did the shooting, "We bought one."

What happens next is as old as the oldest slave narrative.

Three black con men who have been involved in the murder of a crooked white man take flight. In Nebraska, Robert notices a sign and ruminates, "When I saw the sign saying Lincoln I remembered school and the lesson on states and capitals. Maybe it was something about Lincoln freeing the slaves. . . . I was happy I seen that Lincoln sign."

John Wideman's flight is of a different nature. Like Toni Morrison's memorable New Woman, Jadine, he is in flight from his background and from his "community." He is alienated from his roots and from the "jitterbug" styles that embarrass him. He constructs a shell around himself. He hides his inner feelings. "I'd come West to escape the demons Robby personified. I didn't need outlaw brothers reminding me how much had been lost, how much compromised, how terribly the world still raged beyond the charmed circle of my life on the Laramie plains."

On February 13, 1976, the day after the three fugitives take refuge in John Wideman's home in Laramie, they are arrested in Fort Collins, Colorado. John reports that one detective described the captives as "Niggers wanted for Murder One back East." What happened to Robert Wideman after his arrest is all too familiar in a country where one finds a disproportionate number of black males in jail, in the army, or in the morgue as homicide victims. He spent six months in jail before going to trial, and two years in a county jail before receiving a sentence. According to John, the jury was given a "prejudiced charge" by the trial judge; despite that, Robert's appeal was denied by the Supreme Court of Pennsylvania.

Although *Brothers and Keepers* is, above all, a sensitive and intimate portrayal of the lives and divergent paths taken by two brothers, John Wideman's visits to prison are the source of some powerfully written scenes in which he conveys his impressions of American prisons. He never allows his narrative to become merely a sociological tract on prison reform, but he does share his insights concerning a society that would allow the abominable conditions existing inside prisons. Particularly vivid are his experiences with the guards, "the Keepers," who humiliate the prisoners and degrade their guests with lurid-minded strip searches: "You say it's a wire in your bra, lady. Well, I'm sorry but you gotta take it off."

Occasionally, the guards promote or carry out death sentences against prisoners they consider to be "troublemakers." Mr. Wideman refers to one guard as a "Nazi Gestapo Frankenstein robot," a characterization that might disappoint those who see the author as merely another bland, genteel, malleable and mumbling token writer and professor. The guards aren't the only ones who receive Mr. Wideman's verbal hornet strings. Here is his description of the prison waiting room: "The room made me feel like a bug in the bottom of a jar. I remembered all the butterflies, grasshoppers, praying mantises, and beetles I had captured on the hillside below the tracks. At least the insects could see through the glass walls, at least they could flutter or hop or fly, and they always had enough air until I unscrewed the perforated top and dumped them out."

Mr. Wideman remembers times in his life when he wanted to punch or to murder someone instead of tolerating the insults. In *Black Like Me*, John Howard Griffin, the white journalist who "passed" for black in order to see how it felt, wrote that the rudeness and hostility that black men faced in everyday life were what surprised him the most. Mr. Wideman was almost thrown in jail himself for being an accomplice to the crime committed by his brother and his friends, and he was questioned about his possible involvement in another robbery that his brother was suspected of. "I was black. My brother was a suspect. So perhaps I was the fourth perpetrator. No matter that I lived four hundred miles from the scene of the crime. No matter that I wrote books and taught literature and creative writing at the university. I was black. Robby was my brother. Those unalterable facts would always incriminate me."

Having toured a number of American jails, including Attica and San Quentin, as a writing instructor for inmates, I wholeheartedly agree with Mr. Wideman's estimate of American prisons. Indeed, one could say that his precocious daughter is too polite when she compares the jail where she visits her Uncle Robby to a cage where animals are kept. Mr. Wideman may be off-target, however, when he suggests that the conditions in jails are solely the fault of the keepers. Ultimately, the guards do not set policy. Underpaid and ill trained, they are merely sullen gray knights who carry out the policies of others. During the uprising at Attica, both prisoner and guard were slaughtered, achieving in death a kind of ironic camaraderie. But when Mr. Wideman compares the situation of the inmates in prison to that of "civil death," he will find little disagreement from those who have actually taken time to visit a prison, a trip I recommend to some of our intellectual armchair experts who believe that human rights violations are what happen only in "backward" parts of the world. For Mr. Wideman, visiting his brother is like "going to a funeral parlor.

Both situations demand unnatural responses, impose a peculiar discipline on the visitor. . . . You are mourning, bereaved, but you pretend the shell in the coffin is somehow connected with the vital, breathing person you once knew."

Though his life is in constant danger, Robert Wideman refuses to be entombed—for him the prison becomes a monastery. While in prison, he has earned a college degree. John begins to admire his brother and discovers that the same characteristics that landed him in jail help him to survive.

There have been a slew of prison books, especially in the 1960s. Most were written to address the conscience of those in a position to eradicate the ugly, medieval conditions that exist in many American jails. Mr. Wideman says his purpose in writing *Brothers and Keepers* is not to reach the nation's conscience but to reach out to his brother, to "salvage" something "from grief and waste." Still, he is aware of the "political mood of the country." "Keep these misfits away from me" is society's attitude, an attitude that demands more jails, stiffer penalties, and no plea bargaining.

Mr. Wideman uses an impressive array of literary skills in *Brothers and Keepers*. In one passage, he convincingly mimes the rhythms and style of the Depression writings of Carl Sandburg and Margaret Walker: "Wagons once upon a time in the streets of Pittsburgh. Delivering ice and milk and coal. Sinking in the mud, trundling over cobblestones, echoing in the sleep of a man who works all day in the mouth of a fiery furnace, who dreams of green fish gliding along the clear, stony bottom of a creek in South Carolina. In the twenty years between 1910 and 1930, the black population of Pittsburgh increased by nearly fifty thousand. Black music, blues and jazz, came to town in places like the Pythian Temple, the Ritz, the Savoy, the Showboat. In the bars on the North Side, Homewood, and the Hill you could get whatever you thought you wanted. Gambling, women, a good pork chop."

Judging from *Brothers and Keepers*, Robert Wideman is a changed man; he has been rehabilitated. And in his speech printed toward the end of the book, on the occasion of his getting his college degree while in prison, he says: "My education helped me to realize . . . that nothing worth having comes without hard work and concrete effort. But being shaped by the world through this 'quick-get-over' concept and seeing that this concept was folly, it is now time to take our lives and our world in our own hands and shape it for the better." A reason for optimism but, in the last depressing letter from Robert Wideman to his brother, we learn that the program that allowed him to receive his degree has been terminated.

Robert Wideman knows who he is. But John Wideman isn't sure about himself, and his "identity crisis" is the source of the intense, brooding, and brilliant monologues appearing throughout the book as he probes his motives and feelings. "I have a lot to hide," he acknowledges. Like most middle-class ethnic novelists who are partly assimilated Yankee, Mr. Wideman occasionally rebukes himself with harsh and self-deprecating remorse. But one could argue that only from his vantage point, a hazy area between two worlds, is he able to discover original and profound truths about both worlds. W. E. B. Du Bois's "double consciousness" (or even "triple consciousness") is not a dilemma but constitutes a further step in man's intellectual evolution. The terrifying crises of our time have been brought about by the inability of people to put themselves in the other guy's shoes.

Mr. Wideman has succeeded brilliantly in both understanding his brother's life and coming to terms with his own. He has no reason for remorse.

Dream Ticket

Despite his gallant and civilized attempt to win the presidency, Walter Mondale has been criticized by a number of columnists for his inability to control what they call special-interest groups. For the Democrats to regain the support of white males, more than sixty percent of whom voted for the Republican ticket, they argue, the Democrats must cease to be the party of wimps, a reputation they acquired during the campaign of 1984.

The Democrats can accomplish this in 1988 by nominating two men who've proved that they will have no truck with minorities and "San Francisco Democrats," a ticket that will woo the white Chrysler-convertible-driving fraternity brothers and the he-men who boil beans in the kitchens of their Winnebagos and shoot bears from helicopters.

By nominating Bernhard Hugo Goetz for president and former San Francisco Supervisor Dan White* for vice president, the Democrats will send a clear signal to millions of virile Americans that the party is abreast of the times, no longer a dispenser of milky, outdated New Deal mush.

*Mr. White committed suicide on October 22, 1986. My substitute dream vice presidential candidate would be Lt. Col. Oliver North.

Goetz became a hero to millions of potential voters by shooting four young blacks—two of them in the back—when they "accosted" him by asking for five dollars. According to early news reports, three were carrying sharpened screwdrivers, though New York *Daily News* columnist Jimmy Breslin said on the CNN show "Crossfire" that the screwdrivers weren't sharpened. As for those who felt that Goetz's reaction was way out of proportion to the crime—assuming it can be established that a crime was committed—well, what do you expect from those epicene supporters of secular humanism and other wimpy philosophies?

Dan White showed his opposition to the weak-sister political ideas of the Democratic Left by assassinating Harvey Milk, a gay Supervisor, and Mayor George Moscone, a charismatic Democrat who brought the locked-out into San Francisco City Hall. Some say that had he lived, Moscone would have become Governor of California or a candidate for national office.

White's lawyer said that the defendant, who finished off Moscone while he lay wounded from earlier gunshot wounds, killed the two men because he had eaten too many Twinkies. The Democrats can expect large contributions to the Goetz-White ticket from the manufacturers of junk food.

The 1988 Republican ticket, composed of Vice President George Bush and Representative Jack Kemp, won't have a chance against Goetz-White. During his debate with Goetz, a poised Bush will display an impressive knowledge of both foreign and domestic affairs. But he will lose the debate in one dramatic moment when Goetz will turn to him and say, "You only tried to kick a little ass; I went out and burned some." Bush will have no rejoinder, and in his network commentary following the debate, George Will will award the debate to Goetz and will describe his dramatic flourish as truly Hobbesian.

Although the Republicans will run on a complicated platform, Goetz and White will be vague about theirs, or limit themselves to a couple of promises. Maybe the Army of God will be appointed to screen all potential Supreme Court nominees, that is if we need a Supreme Court. Hell, what's wrong with the law of the jungle?

As for foreign policy, Grenada already having been occupied, maybe the pair will promise to send the marines into Berkeley, California, to take care of those City Council members who are reluctant to salute the flag.

If support for the Goetz-White ticket falls off as Election Day approaches, the team can always galvanize the voters by staging some sort of electrifying event. Perhaps Goetz can shoot some young black patrons of a video-game arcade, saying he was once accosted there, or, if he wants to take the high road and leave the hatchet job—or shall we say trigger job—to his vice presidential nominee, White can always get loaded on candy, sneak into the basement window of some city hall, and correct a left-leaning mayor the way he corrected George Moscone, who didn't even have a screwdriver to protect himself.

The Republicans will spend millions on their campaign; the Goetz-White ticket will cost very little. A full-page advertisement in the *National Enquirer* with the slogan "You Know Where We Stand," or "Why Not the Worst?" or, a week before the election, "Vote Tuesday: Make Their Day," will do.

President Goetz's first appointment will be George Will as press secretary. During his first news conference, Will will admit that he was the person who suggested that Goetz challenge Bush on who was the better "ass-kicker"—the challenge that some will say gave the debate, and thus the election, to Goetz. Will will then comment on the morality of the new "state of nature" administration, quoting seventeenth-century British philosopher Thomas Hobbes, who was also a bootlicker for royalty. In a wink at traditional values, Washington will be renamed Dodge City, but the biggest surprise will come after pollsters analyze the voting trends. The black backlash that was expected against Goetz and White will have failed to materialize. Millions of blacks like Clint Eastwood, too.

How the Afrikaners
Can Hold On

Only by watching the recent television performance of President Botha can one appreciate the new-wave racism operating in other parts of the world. Separated from their fellow racists for a few hundred years, it's obvious the Afrikaners have not kept up with state-of-the-art apartheid.

Compare Mr. Botha's outdated "separate development" with the slick, high-tech "constructive engagement." Whoever invented that phrase must have been a genius, as the man on the grapes commercial says.

Mr. Botha and his followers have not learned the art of appearing to make radical reforms while at the same time maintaining the status quo.

First, he should give blacks the right to vote, but instruct his attorney general to refuse any federal protection for enforcing those rights. Use gerrymandering, annexation, reapportionment, and dual primaries to frustrate majority rule.

Desegregate public education, but send out signals to your fellow Afrikaners that you will use federal funds to finance private schools for the education of their children.

Agree to affirmative action as a means of redressing the past injustices to blacks, but instruct your attorney general to challenge these actions in court. Set up a civil rights commission, but choose to head it with nonwhites who you know share your values. Have them declare the society "color blind."

Deny the blacks access to capital through redlining, etc., and then have your friends in the media say blacks themselves are responsible for their lack of prosperity. Pay a black economist a couple of rands to say they've always been lazy. Use the same black economist to compare the blacks unfavorably with the Indian South Africans. Announce the Indians are model nonwhites.

Train Mr. Botha to use television better. Buy him an airbrushed toupee and contact lenses. Get him to improve his jokes. The one about the skunk lacked finesse.

And for heaven's sake, tell him to stop showing his anger and getting into low-class confrontations with his hecklers, during which he is consistently outwitted. This looks bad for an international audience. He should smile more. He can even smile while threatening his enemies. Have him practice by saying, "You ain't seen nothin' yet" with a smile.

Champion*

*T*his outstanding book not only chronicles the career of a great boxer but charts the rise of sports as a legitimate form of American recreation and the public's changing perceptions of the Afro-American athlete, the traditional symbol for Afro-Americans themselves.

Chris Mead's *Champion*, subtitled *Joe Louis, Black Hero in White America*, tells the story of Joe Louis from his discovery by manager Jack Blackburn and owner John Roxborough to his death on April 12, 1981. After "White America's" bitter reaction to the career of heavyweight champion Jack Johnson, Mr. Blackburn, a numbers man, insisted that Joe Louis live an exemplary life so that "White America" would accept another black heavyweight champion.

Being on his best behavior didn't work. Sportswriters continued to use jungle imagery when describing Louis, to use an Uncle Remus minstrel accent when quoting him, and to question his discipline.

The first big break of his boxing career came when he defeated Primo Carnera on June 25, 1935. According to Mead,

*A review of *Champion: Joe Louis, Black Hero in White America*, by Chris Mead, Charles Scribner's Sons, 1986

this fight "catapulted Louis to public prominence." As a result, Joe Louis became the most famous black person in history.

The most dramatic portions of the book deal with the fights and rematches that Louis had with Max Schmeling and Billy Conn. Schmeling, who noticed the same flaw in Louis's style that Jack Johnson had spotted, knocked Louis out in the first fight. Through the negotiating skill of his rags-to-riches owner, Max Jacobs, Louis was able to fight the reigning champion, James Braddock, despite the setback at Schmeling's fists. His defeat of Braddock on June 22, 1937, made him the youngest heavyweight ever to win the championship.

This was still not enough for Louis to win the acceptance of "White America," which had rooted for Schmeling, a Nazi who dined with Adolph Hitler. It was only after Louis defeated Schmeling the second time—by then a symbol of Nazi imperialism—entered the army, and donated his money to the navy and army, did "White America" grudgingly begin to accept him as a human being. Paul Gallico, who had described Louis as "cruel, savage, and primitive," wrote, "He has won respect." But his owner's attempt to please "White America" led to Louis's downfall. His indebtedness to his wife, Jacobs, and to the Internal Revenue Service among others accumulated, and the absence of lucrative fights during his army career caused these debts to enslave him. After his discharge from the army, he had to continue to fight in order to satisfy his creditors. Even after his knockout by Rocky Marciano, Louis contemplated a comeback in order to satisfy debts that by the end of his career had become astronomical. He became a wrestler in order to earn money and finally took a job in a casino. Introduced to cocaine by a mysterious woman, ac-

cording to Louis, he suffered from occasional bouts of para-
noia.

Millions of people used Joe Louis to gain prestige without
having to exert any effort on their own parts. He was for them
and for his camp followers a walking freebie, a patsy, a mark.
The white sportswriters and their readers used Louis as an
African beast, next to whom they could appear civilized and
refined; the blacks used him as a symbol of how well behaved
they could be and as a way of taking revenge against "White
America," which for them was symbolized by Louis's opponents. (There's no evidence that Joe Louis, who coined America's World War II battle cry, "God Is On Our Side," was a
racist. When Rocky Marciano died, a picture of Louis, leaning
over the late champion's casket, sobbing, appeared in the black
weekly *Jet*.) After his defeat of Max Schmeling, he was used
as a symbol of democracy. His greedy manager, Max Jacobs,
used him to get rich. His first wife, Marva, used him to elevate
herself to the position of a black queen. Joe Louis was used
and used, until he was all used up, but even as a Las Vegas
greeter he possessed more class than those who exploited him.

Predictably, Mr. Mead dismisses criticism that Louis was
not qualified to speak for "Black America," presumably because these criticisms were made by the black middle class, a
class that comes in for considerable criticism from middle-
class white and black writers.

More of a lovable fool than an Uncle Tom, the man whom
"White America" viewed as a big brown teddy bear had militant confrontations with armed white racists while a member
of the segregated armed forces. Some of these conflicts, according to Mead, led to better conditions for black soldiers.

Mead gives credit to Louis for forcing whites to face their racism, thus opening the door for the civil rights movement.

After reading Chris Mead's thorough and compelling book, one gains respect for the dignified Joe Louis as well as for the "arrogant" Jack Johnson, whose image Louis's owners sought to eclipse. If, as some scientists and scholars claim, racism is a mental-health problem, then one could argue that Johnson (despised by Mead's "White America") refused to live his life according to the requirements of sick and unfortunate people.

In Opposition — Which State?

T he civil rights movement not only led to political reforms in the United States, but inspired a multiethnic revival in literature. No longer was the main concern of many Afro-American writers that of imitating the prevailing literary styles, but of setting the styles of the oral tradition to the page and delivering poetry from the drawing room to the streets. The use of Black English, and for other nonwhite ethnic groups, Yellow English, Brown English, and Red English, inspired a controversy that has not ceased. In fact, Robert Burchfield, in his book *The English Language*, writes that it wasn't until the seventies that critics began to bemoan the decline of English —a language that has undergone, in Burchfield's words, "remarkable" and "irreversible" changes since Old English, changes that have occurred, up to the seventies, he continues, "without the expression by contemporaries of any degree of hostility, and even without comment of any kind."

Many critics have denounced the multiethnic revival that occurred in the 1960s with the arrival of a new generation of Afro-American, Asian American, Native American, and Hispanic writers. Some have been denouncing it as a fad for over a decade. In fact, we've passed the twentieth anniversary from the time that the first hostile reactions against the multiethnic revival began to appear in print; the controversy continues as the multiethnic revival expands.

Responses to the multiethnic revival by mainstream literary institutions have been to greet it with silence, cultivate ethnic tokens to denounce it, or denounce it, deny that it exists, yet borrow from it, a tactic that Cherokee critic Geary Hobson describes as "cultural imperialism"; he uses the phrase to discuss what he calls "white shamans," those white male writers who deceived the reading public into thinking that they were "Indians" when they were, in fact, as one critic said, "Boy Scouts dressed up as Indians." Some of the most bitter comments concerning the multiethnic revival have originated in the American avant-garde, those who believe that aesthetic manifestos long ago faded into the cabaret walls of Europe are a new discovery. Currently there is much talk in their publications about jazz writing, which they say began with experiments in North Beach, San Francisco in the 1950s; Langston Hughes and other pioneers produced jazz, bebop, and blues writing in the thirties and forties. (Blues verse is the United States's most popular literary export; one doesn't hear T. S. Eliot reading "The Wasteland" in the cafes of Europe and Martinique, but John Lee Hooker.)

A typical expression of cultural imperialism occurred when a critic for the *New York Times* recently wrote that the possibility for "rock and roll" as high art only occurred when Bobby Dylan began to write rock and roll, an Afro-American invention.

Whether the multiethnic revival constitutes an American renaissance as some have claimed, or is composed of writers who lack "standards," "quality," or "universality," one cannot deny its tenacity.

Despite the neglect of Hispanic writers by the literary mainstream, books by Hispanic writers are still being published, mostly by small presses. Hundreds of books have been published by Native American authors in the last ten years, so that American readers don't have to rely upon anthropologists or Anglo middlepersons for knowledge about Native American life. Shawn Wong, the first Asian American male writer to publish a novel in the United States, said that in 1970 few Asian Americans could name an Asian American author, but recently at Suzanne Zavrian's New York Book Fair, held at Madison Square Garden, there were enough Asian American authors to fill an entire day of programming.

In 1985, Schocken Books published an anthology of writings by Italian American women entitled *The Dream Book*. Helen Barolini, the anthologist, included women who share a common heritage and cited the black writers as an inspiration for such an anthology.

In our effort to acquaint American and foreign readers with the diversity of American literature, the literature of Asian American, Native American, Hispanic, and white ethnic writers, we receive either opposition or indifference, not from the state administered by politicians, but from the other state, the literary state. Indeed, the politicians' state, through such programs as the National Endowment for the Arts, has a better record for recognizing multiethnic literature than does the literary state.

It's been over twenty years since Walter Lowenfels, one of our best poets, complained about "the white literary mob," yet we still have anthologists who use the terms "American," and "National," but print only "whites" and maybe a few tokens from time to time. We still have all-white literary juries deciding who gets fellowships, grants, and prizes. We still have major literary organizations that include few Afro-Americans, Asian Americans, Native Americans, and Hispanics. The administrators of these organizations should be alarmed by the fact that the current administration, a regime they consider to be right-wing, includes, on the average, more nonwhites in its ranks than the country's leading literary organizations.

The current literary establishment, which denies that it exists, is not only a powerful influence upon American intellectual and cultural trends but on political trends as well— both the left wing and right wing of the New York branch having advised political administrations since the 1960s. It is in a position to influence the perception of American literature held by foreign readers, writers, and literary institutions. If any deny this fact, I would invite them to inspect the books selected by a committee formed by the Association of American Publishers that was sent to the 1985 Moscow Book Fair as a part of an exhibit called "America Through American Eyes." Our eyes weren't included. True to its devotion to tokenism, the committee, which reflected the literary establishment's tastes, included only one Hispanic and one Native American writer. Afro-American writers were represented mostly by right-wing feminists who believe in some of the same racial theories as the Ku Klux Klan. It's bad enough that foreigners obtain their information about Afro-American life from a neoconservative producer's "Hill Street Blues," but now we're going to be judged by *The Color Purple*, the motion picture version of which has inspired the worst campaign of group libel against black men since the days of the Confederate writers. The list didn't include a single Afro-American, Asian American, or

Hispanic poet, male or female, but someone thought enough to include *Jane Fonda's Workout Book.*

Recently, delegations of mostly white members and their tokens traveled to the Soviet Union and to China. No Chinese American male writer was included in the delegation. One of the delegates complained about cultural repression in both countries but when called upon to describe literary trends in the United States cited only the white male members of his club.

The problem with the current literary-industrial complex of publishers, critics, writers, and slowpoke academia is that it can see cultural repression when it happens in other states but can't recognize it when it's practiced by its own state, the literary state. By providing not only American readers but foreign readers with an incomplete view of a complex literary scene, dismissing not only multiethnic writers but regional writers—with such put-down phrases as "hick chic"—these literary institutions are guilty of the same thing.

In 1976, ten years ago, a group of white and nonwhite ethnic writers decided that, instead of engaging in a time and energy consuming confrontation with the commercial literary institutions, we could best serve the literature we championed by establishing new institutions. We began the Before Columbus Foundation, devoted to the promotion of multiethnic literatures. The Before Columbus Foundation distributes books and magazines published by more than two hundred multiethnic presses and, beginning last year, represented these presses at international book fairs in Frankfurt, Cairo, and Moscow through the efforts of an organization named the Soviet American Book Exchange. We provided Soviet readers with an alternative to *Jane Fonda's Workout Book.*

In 1978, the Before Columbus Foundation originated the American Book Awards as a way of recognizing the United States' diverse literatures, but since a few years later a Wall Street version of the American Book Awards was begun, our activities, though covered in Asian, African, and European media—including the *London Times*—have been ignored by the American mass media, which seem to prefer conflict between white and nonwhite ethnics to cooperation. Recently they've sought to promote Asian Americans as the model minority, lumping diverse groups together as usual, as a way of "dividing and conquering," a phrase used by Japanese American and Chinese American writers and scholars to describe this cynical effort. The American media pretend to love what they refer to as Asian Americans, but seldom do they review their literary efforts or print articles written by Asian Americans.

Celebrating a truly peoples' book award, the American Book Award ceremonies have been held in Berkeley, San Francisco, and New York. This year's book awards will be held in New Orleans, and the city of Philadelphia will host the 1987 American Book Awards as part of that city's two hundredth anniversary.

Though we have a board of directors that includes Irish Americans, Italian Americans, Jewish Americans, Native Americans, Asian Americans, Hispanics, Afro-Americans, and feminists, our critics dismiss us as "Third World" or "minority" when we include more white ethnics in our organization—which last year sponsored a panel of Italian American writers at the Museo-Italo Americano in San Francisco—than they do nonwhites on their all-white juries, committees, and lists of books recommended for foreign consumption, and in their all-white anthologies. If for them ethnicity means of limited concerns, then who is ethnic? Who is narrow? Our eyes or their "America-Through-American-Eyes" list, which included only one publisher from west of the Rockies?

As a way of relieving some of our best multicultural artists, writers, and scholars from the burden of many ethnic studies departments begrudgingly added to university curricula by traditionalists—programs that are hampered by lack of funds and the resulting rivalry—we established the Before Columbus Institute so that writers from different backgrounds would not be segregated from one another but would team-teach poetry and prose, presenting students with the varieties of literature that have been produced in America, not merely that of the monoethnic canon.

We are not in opposition to the literary state; we'd like to enter into a dialogue with it. We'd like to cooperate with it. We'd like it to join us in projecting the United States as a planet-nation—a nation that is generated by diversity and cultural exchange between people from different backgrounds. What the brilliant young critic Greg Tate calls "horizontal integration." It is they who are knowingly, or unknowingly, in opposition to our vision, and this situation undermines their efforts to communicate with writers and literary institutions in the rest of the world, for how can they know and understand foreign cultures when they know little about us and are still dependent upon synopses of our cultures provided by their tokens, who tell them what they want to hear? How can they maintain their snooty attitudes toward the politicians' state, calling politicians ideologues, when they are just as closed-minded to the changes that have occurred in American literature? How can they abide a situation in which European scholars, writers, and artists—whose intellectual trends they imitate, and whose intellectual traditions didn't just begin fifty years ago—know more about the writing scene in the United States, multiethnic and regional, than they do?

In Frankfurt, Germany, last summer I met scholars who were specialists in Chinese American and Native American writers. The American literary industrial complex seems to be only aware of one or two from each of these groups.

Foreign writers, scholars, and critics have done much to make readers in their countries aware of the multiethnic revival that is happening in this country. They can also help us by requesting that the all-white American delegations sent by American political and cultural institutions to Africa, Asia, and Europe be replaced by those which more accurately reflect the United States' diverse literature.

We are not crude writers engaged in ugly rhetoric against things we disapprove of. We're merely requesting that the literary industrial complex face up to the important changes that have occurred in American literature since the 1960s.

Hyped or Hip?*

*B*y the time Chester Himes reached the age of nineteen, he'd suffered more misfortune than most people experience in a lifetime, including a fall down an elevator shaft that left him permanently disabled and an accident in a chemistry lab, for which he was partially responsible, that left his brother Joseph blinded.

Seeking better medical treatment for Himes's brother, the Himes family traveled from St. Louis to Cleveland, where Himes was introduced to the criminal underworld. After his expulsion from Ohio State University for taking some coeds to a brothel, Himes became a pimp, a car thief, a gambler, and an illegal-guns merchant, which accounts for the familiarity with weapons the author uses in his detective novels. ("They had .303 automatic Savage rifles leaded with .190-point brass-nosed shells, equipped with telescopic sights.") On December 27, 1928, Himes was sentenced to twenty to twenty-five years of hard labor in the Ohio State Penitentiary for stealing jewels from a wealthy couple. He entered prison at nineteen and didn't leave until he was twenty-six.

*A review of A *Rage in Harlem*; *Cotton Comes to Harlem*; *The Crazy Kill*; *The Real Cool Killers*, by Chester Himes, Allison and Busby, 1986

A monthly disability check from the hotel where his near-fatal accident took place enabled him to avoid prison labor, and so he devoted his time to writing and gambling, a knowledge that he would bring to his future detective fiction. ("In Georgia Skin the suits—spades, hearts, clubs, and diamonds —have no rank. The cards are played by denomination. There are thirteen denominations in the deck, the ace through the king. Therefore, thirteen cards must be played.") His first literary efforts were published between 1931 and 1934 in the *Pittsburgh Courier*, the *Atlantic Daily World*, *Abbott's Monthly Magazine*, and *Esquire*.

It was his experience as a gangster and a convict that prepared Chester Himes, son of a college teacher and a mother fair enough to pass for white, to become—in the estimation of some critics—the United States' premier detective novelist. But, ironically, it wasn't until many years after his departure from prison, during his exile, that Himes began to write his famous Harlem detective series. He said he got the idea from Marcel Duhamel, then director of Gallimard's detective-story series, *La Série Noire*, who suggested to Himes that he "get an idea, start with action, somebody does something—a man reaches out a hand and opens a door, light shines in his eyes, a body lies on the floor, he turns, looks up and down the hall. . . . Always action in detail. Make pictures. Like motion pictures. Always the scenes are visible. No stream of consciousness at all. We don't give a damn who's thinking what —only what they're doing. Always doing something. From one scene to another. Don't worry about it making sense."

His first detective novel, *La Reine des Pommes* (The Five-Cornered Square), was published in 1957 and was the 1958 winner of Le Grand Prix Roman Policier.

As one of the few Afro-American writers to break into the detective genre, Himes was regarded as a celebrity in Europe; his knowledge of Harlem and his familiarity with the American urban underworld made these novels unique. Himes wasn't just making up fiction for the entertainment of mystery-hungry fans; he was writing from experience. Even some of the names of the characters who appear in the detective novels are based on people he knew during his gangster days, including Red Johnny, Four Four, Chink Charlie, Dummy, and Abie the Jew, who appears in *A Rage in Harlem*. As a craftsman, Himes had few peers. His scenes, characterizations, dialogue, and his absurdist point of view—a point of view he traced to Albert Camus, but one that can be found in Afro-American folklore—contributed to these novels becoming the classics that they are. In Himes's gangster view of the world, people are either hyped or hip, had or not had. Not only do hustlers promote bogus gold mines but political platforms as well. In *Cotton Comes to Harlem*, Back to Africa and Back to the South are schemes that both black and white gangsters use in order to steal $87,000 collected from the poor. In *A Rage In Harlem*, an undertaker's employee succumbs to a scam known as The Blow.

In The Blow, a sucker is introduced to a "scientist," who claims he can raise a low-denomination bill to a higher de-nomination: for example, a ten to a hundred. While the sucker is watching a "demonstration," to which he has brought all of his money, a fake U.S. marshal interrupts the demonstra-tion, allows the scientist to escape, and arrests the sucker. The fake marshal settles for a bribe from the sucker; the marshal and scientist, who are partners, move on to the next town.

Religion is also used as a racket, which fits Himes's philosophy that all men ultimately are corrupt. ("There was something about raising the denomination of money that appealed to the larceny in men," the narrator comments in A *Rage in Harlem*.) Even the heroes of these novels, detectives Coffin Ed Johnson and Grave Digger Jones, are on the take. People dressed as nuns and known as the Sisters of Mercy collect money from the unsuspecting; the Real Cool Moslems of *The Real Cool Killers* are a gang of hoodlums who supply a white sadist with young Harlem girls, including Sugartit, Coffin Ed's daughter (when he discovers this, his partner, Grave Digger, nearly beats a punk to death and has to be restrained).

Christopher Lehmann-Haupt made a very perceptive comment about Himes's style when he described him as a writer with "enormous capacity to record sensuous life as it is experienced from one moment to the next." Not only do we see, hear, and taste the Harlem of Himes's novels but the smells as well:

"The blue-gray air was thick as split-pea soup with tobacco smoke, pungent with the scent of cheap perfume and hothouse lillies, the stink of sweating bodies, the fumes of alcohol, hot fried food and bad breath."

Instead of carrying his criticism of types and institutions in a heavy-handed narrative, Himes slips his in during the description of a character: "Reverend Gaines fingered the satin lapel of his blue flannel smoking-jacket. The diamond of his third finger sparkled in the light." Social protest is delivered in a character's speech; he has one of his heroes say, " 'I'm just a cop. . . . If you white people insist on coming to Harlem where you force colored people to live in vice- and crime-ridden slums, it's my job to see that you are safe.' . . . The white man turned bright red." Not that Himes succumbed to the temptation to paint all black people as good and all white people as bad, the kind of primary notions that often mar good novels. Himes played no favorites. In his autobiography he wrote: "Maybe it was an unconscious protest against soul brothers always being considered as victims of racism, a protest against racism itself excusing all their sins and major faults. Black victims of crime and criminals might be foolish and harebrained, but the soul brother criminals were as vicious, cruel and dangerous as any other criminals—I knew because I'd been one—the only difference being they were absurd."

His attempts to get inside the mind of Coffin Ed's and Grave Digger's commander, Lieutenant Anderson, a white, are sympathetic and convincing. In *Cotton Comes to Harlem* he writes of Lieutenant Anderson: "He looked white about the gills himself. It had been a hot, raw night—Independence night, he thought—filled with big and little crime. He was sick of crime and criminals; sick of both cops and robbers, sick of Harlem and colored people. He liked colored people all right; they couldn't help it because they were colored. He was quite attached to his two ace detectives; in fact he depended on them. They probably kept his job for him. He was second in command to the precinct captain, and had charge of the night shift. He was the sole responsibility when the captain went home, and without his two aces he might not have been able to carry it. Harlem was a mean rough city and you had to be meaner and rougher to keep any kind of order. He understood why colored people were mean and rough; he'd be mean and rough himself if he was colored. He understood all the evils of segregation. He sympathized with the colored people in his precinct, and with colored people in general. But right now he was good and goddamned sick of them. All he wanted was to go home to his quiet house in Queens in a quiet white neighborhood and kiss his white wife and look in on his two sleeping white children and crawl into bed between two white sheets and go the hell to sleep."

Though Himes was an intelligent reader of the modernists—his criticisms of Faulkner are shrewd—he didn't slavishly imitate them, as did some of his Afro-American contemporaries; his style most resembles that of the urban toast, the chief literary form of entertainment in American prisons —rhymed verses about the lives of hustlers and whores characterized by irony, comedy, humor, and hyperbole. Take this description of a woman in A *Rage in Harlem*, which comes as close as we're likely to get to the jazz prose American avant-garde writers are striving to achieve: "She was a cushion-lipped, hot-bodied, banana-skin chick with the speckled-brown eyes of a teaser and the high-arched, ball-bearing hips of a natural-born amante"; or the description of a gambler, Big Joe, in *The Crazy Kill*: "Big Joe was dressed in a cream-colored Palm Beach suit, pale green crepe de chine shirt, brown silk tie with hand-painted angels held in place by a diamond horseshoe stickpin." His heroes, Coffin Ed Johnson and Grave Digger Jones, don't dress as extravagantly. In fact, in *The Real Cool Killers* we learn that "they looked like big-shouldered plow-hands in Sunday suits at a Saturday night jamboree." With the creation of these characters, Himes risked and received the condemnation of alienated black intellectuals, who were horrified by their values—the values of the working black middle-class, of which Grave Digger and Coffin Ed were products. They are realists. They are family men. They live in middle-class neighborhoods in Astoria, Queens. They like jazz and know about black Shakespearean actors like Canada Lee, but their methods for dealing with criminals, though repellent to those they would call sob sisters, are effective and often brutal.

"Ever since the hoodlum had thrown acid into his face [an incident that occurs in *A Rage in Harlem*], Coffin Ed had no tolerance for crooks. He was quick to blow up and too dangerous for safety in his sudden rages. But hell, Grave Digger thought, what can one expect? These colored hoodlums had no respect for colored cops unless you beat it into them or blew them away."

Whatever their methods, the hoodlums respect the detectives so much that they sheepishly obey the pair who maneuver them through military drills. These drills, which occur in more than one of Himes's books, have amused and delighted generations of Himes's working-class readers: "Grave Digger stood on the right side of the front end of the line, at the entrance to the Savoy. Coffin Ed stood on the left side of the line, at the rear end. Grave Digger had his pistol aimed south, in a straight line down the sidewalk. On the other side, Coffin Ed had his pistol aimed north, in a straight line. There was space enough between the two imaginary lines for two persons to stand side by side. Whenever anyone moved out of line, Grave Digger would shout, 'Straighten up!' and Coffin Ed would echo, 'Count off!' If the offender didn't straight up the line immediately, one of the detectives would shoot into the air."

Chester Himes was very bitter when he left the United States for Europe on April 3, 1953. He decided to leave after the reception to his book *Lonely Crusade*, which was based on his experiences as a machine worker and a draftsman in the Los Angeles and Richmond, California war industries. "The Left hated it, the Right hated it, the Jews hated it, blacks hated it. . . ." He accused the Communist party of having sabotaged the book commercially. Black writers Willard Motley and James Baldwin came down hard on it. His friend Richard Wright was lukewarm. Of his motives for writing *Lonely Crusade*, Himes wrote, "I had attempted to be completely fair. I had written what I thought was a story of the fear that inhabits the minds of blacks who live in America and the various impacts on this fear precipitated by communism, industrialism, unionism, the war, white women, and marriage within the race. It was not too big a scope; this was our daily life during the war. I did not record a single event that I hadn't known to happen; the characters were people who either had lived or could have lived; the situations were commonplace."

Abroad, Himes achieved a celebrity and critical acclaim denied to him in the United States. Jean Giono said, "I give you all of Hemingway, Dos Passos and Fitzgerald for this Chester Himes."

It wasn't until the early 1970s, when Doubleday published his autobiography, *The Quality of Hurt*, and Samuel Goldwyn, Jr. bought the rights to do what would become successful films, *Cotton Comes to Harlem* and *Come Back Charleston Blue* (adapted from the novel *The Heat's On*), that Himes received recognition in the United States.

Though disabled by a series of strokes, Chester Himes and his devoted wife, Lesley, managed to visit the United States for the last time in the summer of 1980. Writer Floyd Salas and I greeted them at the airport with flowers. He was celebrated by the Northern California literary community. He didn't talk very much, but the wit and the mischief were still there. I remember the gleam in his eyes, that which Carl Van Vechten captured in one of his portraits of Himes, when Lesley recounted how he'd recently run into trouble with Spanish courts for engaging members of the police force in a gun battle. He'd mistaken them for burglars. "It was the kind of gun you'd shoot an elephant with," Lesley said. Bad contracts with publishers had left Himes in need of funds during his last years. As a nominator for a foundation with billions at its disposal, I tried to obtain a grant for Chester. Instead, the money went to members of the permanent graduate school that's done so much to turn American poetry into gibberish and alienate the average reader and student from verse. Unlike Himes's friend, the intellectually daring and political hot potato Richard Wright, who died under mysterious circumstances surrounded by enemies, Himes managed to survive his critics and to see the country that hurt him so honor him, however belatedly.

The Tradition of
Serious Comedy in
Afro-American
Literature

E very nation has its version of Genesis (the tales of which weren't written until the tenth century), but unlike the biblical Genesis, the myths, legends, and stories of many other nations have yet to be written. This written or oral literature of a nation is often treated with reverence, because it forms the lore of a people. When the Icelandic Sagas were returned to Iceland from Denmark, a public holiday was declared. Similarly, the discovery of the Finnish Kalevala became an occasion of excitement and celebration. The HooDoo stories, the "toasts," and the riddles and other neo-African literary forms constitute the basis for the Afro-American oral tradition, traces of which can be found wherever African people settled in this hemisphere. (Lest some believe that oral literature is somehow inferior to written literature, be they reminded that among the ancient Greeks and Hebrews there waged a debate about whether written literature was a blessing or a curse.)

Employing styles associated with Afro-American culture, styles which I have referred to as "neo-HooDooism," can often invite misunderstanding in a society whose intellectual and cultural leaderships embrace ambivalent attitudes toward Afro-American culture.

Although Afro-American musical styles like jazz and tap

dance, rock and roll, and Black English—a literary style—are regularly used by the commercial world, from time to time campaigns are undertaken whose purpose is to purge the society of such forms. Right now rap music, a descendant of the toast, and rock and roll are being excoriated from the pulpits of televangelists, which is not to say that all of the opponents of Afro-American culture are religious fanatics; indeed, some of the most strident condemnations of Afro-American culture— music, literature, and dance—have originated among the American intelligentsia.

Take, for example, the confusing details regarding Afro-American culture as defined by different sections of the *New York Times*. In an article printed in the *New York Times* music section entitled "African Pop," a critic wrote, "Recognizable Yoruba [Nigerian-based] elements are prominent in salsa and in other music with Cuban roots, and the system of black American religious and magical beliefs known as voodoo or hoodoo is primarily Yoruba-derived."

In the magazine section on August 21, 1983, Warren Hoge wrote an informed article about African-derived culture in this hemisphere. Included in his description of the Brazilian "cult," as he called it, of Macumba is a mention of novelist Jorge Amado, one of the "cult's" followers.

Yet in a letter to the editor dated April 1982, Leonard Feldman responded to an editorial entitled "VooDoo Economics," a title in which voodoo was seen to be synonymous with the ridiculous. He wrote: "The fact is that voodoo is an authentic religion, albeit an exotic one to most Americans, with an established cosmogony, rituals, ceremonies, etc. and its mysteries are no more worthy of mockery than those of any other faith." Undaunted, however, an April 1986 issue of the *New*

York Times Book Review introduced a review of Charles Johnson's *Sorcerer's Apprentice* with the line: "VooDoo and Subtler Forms."

If the *New York Times* is confused about neo-African religious systems, the inspiration for so much of the hemisphere's dance, painting, and writing, then you can understand the confusion of the average person, or of those who've been trained to adhere to only one tradition.

And so I knew that, when I set out to add fresh interpretations to an ancient Afro-American oral literature by modernizing its styles so as to reach contemporary readers, my work would be greeted with controversy. I knew that some critics, rather than investigate the allusions included in my work, would dismiss the material as arcane, when millions of people in North, South, and Central America, the Caribbean, and Africa are acquainted with the structures I used. (Even though my work includes features one finds in postmodernist writing, within the tradition of Afro-American culture it is quite cautious in comparison to the risk-taking, eccentric, and fantastical work of naive Afro-American folk artists and sculptors.)

If the slaves, for example, enjoyed riddles more than any other form, according to folklorist Virginia Hamilton and others, then among my work would be whodunits with busy plots, and trickster endings as in *Reckless Eyeballing*, a part whodunit in which the first clue is contained in the book's title.

If, according to Afro-American folklore, spirits ride human hosts and are referred to as "horsemen," then I would naturally write a western, here again using the traditional styles of Afro-American folklore but enmeshing such styles with popular forms with which readers could identify.

If there exists a body of mysteries in Afro-American oral

literature, then included among my works would be mysteries like *Mumbo Jumbo*, which is not only a detective novel, but a novel concerning the mysteries, the secrets, of competing civilizations.

If in HooDoo literature the real commingled with the unreal, the natural with the supernatural, then this would be the style used in my work.

If the toasts of the urban ghetto tradition used scatology and earthiness similar to the characteristics found in the Native American oral tradition, the Zuni tales, and the coyote tales, for example, then these are characteristics that I would include in my work.

The type of droll humor that I use has also been a source of controversy, though such humor abounds in the Afro-American oral tradition.

When Michael G. Cooke, writing in his book *Afro-American Literature in the Twentieth Century*, said, "Black humor proved a white phenomenon, and the fabulator's sense of life as unreal and mad, though this might seem highly germane to the black experience, has not really taken hold in black writing," I knew that Mr. Cooke was writing about the "serious," conventional, and usually imitative Afro-American novel, because such a statement cannot be made about the oral tradition, in which one finds a fabulator's world, a surreal world, a world in which the supernatural intrudes upon everyday life, a world of the wicked cackle, the world of black humor, a world that some would consider mad.

When I was a child living in Chattanooga I was fascinated by a painting that hung from the wall of a relative's home. It depicted a luxury liner, the *Titanic*, that had sunk to the bottom of the North Atlantic after colliding with an iceberg.

What on earth was that particular painting doing on the wall of my relative's home? I asked myself for many years. It wasn't until I began to study Afro-American folklore that I learned the reason why. The *Titanic* for Afro-Americans symbolized all the formidable forces that they were up against.

Its passengers were society people; its manufacturers boasted of its invincibility; it was white. Jack Johnson, the best heavyweight champion of the world—considered by the American press to be insolent, but a hero to Afro-Americans—was denied a ticket because of his race. The *Titanic's* accident, a tragedy for many Americans but a source of jubilation for Afro-Americans, inspired one of the most popular toasts of the Afro-American tradition, "And Shine Swan On," in which a fictional Afro-American, working in the boiler room, warns the captain of the ship that the vessel is taking in water, only to be ignored. Shine abandons the ship, and when it becomes apparent that Shine is right and the ship is indeed sinking, the rich passengers plead with Shine to rescue them. They offer money, sex, and other bribes, all of which are ignored by Shine, who replies to their pleas: "Get your ass in the water and swim like me." Written in rhymed couplets, with the profane language characteristic of the toasts, the poem ends with a scene in a Harlem bar where Shine, having survived the shark-infested waters of the North Atlantic, tells of his adventures for the amusement of his fellow bar patrons.

This toast is funny and uses the humor of the gallows, but it makes serious points about hubris, about class, and about race.

The Raven myths of the Pacific Northwest are comic, but they deal with serious subjects: the creation of the world and the origin of Death. The major toast of the Afro-American tradition, "The Signifying Monkey," is comic, but it makes a serious point: how the weak are capable of overcoming the strong through wit. The calypso songs of Trinidad may be comic, but they deal with serious subjects. One of the Jamaican singer Mighty Sparrow's songs is about the Cuban missile crisis, as it was called by the United States. In Haiti they even have a loa, or god of satire, named Ghede, popular among the proletariat, who pokes fun at the establishment and "shows each man his devil."

My work is also comic, but it makes, I feel, serious points about politics, culture, and religion.

In the Afro-American oral tradition, trickster figures with no moral scruples whatsoever, and names like Brer Fox and Brer Rabbit, use cunning and guile to gain power. Even entrapment is used, as in the famous tale of "Tar Baby": a decoy covered with a gummy substance is used to lure Brer Rabbit, who has been stealing his neighbor's crops. If tales of the Tar Baby are the result of an amalgamation of African and Native American lore—Native American and Cherokee Indians worked on the same plantations in Tennessee, and millions of Afro-Americans have a Native American as well as a European ancestry—then perhaps when Native American scholars describe the Native American trickster tradition as an essentially comic tradition, they could be characterizing the Afro-American oral tradition as well.

One of the features that attracted me to Afro-American religious systems as one of the sources of my writing was their cosmopolitan approach to art. There seems to be no room in these systems for intellectual meanness. They could mix with other cultures with no thought of "contamination" or "corruption," but of usefulness. If Catholic saints could function as substitutes for African gods, they were used. In Guadalupe, the gods of the immigrant Indians were added to the neo-African pantheon, and a curry dish, with Indian origins, has become the national dish of this Caribbean country. Regardless of its sensational title, *Voodoo, Africa's Secret Power*, by Gert Chesi, provides photographs that show that Afro-American religious systems have reimmigrated to the West Coast of Africa where they originated. It's as though voodoo, or Vodoun, an African-derived system containing features with no African antecedent, has gone home. The artwork in the book's photos demonstrates clearly that images of European and Asian origin coexist with African images. Among the objects being offered to a Krishna figure is a container of Imperial Leather talc for men.

Just as one does not have to be a follower of Zeus to write poetry based upon Greek mythology or a Druid to make use of Celtic mythology, the Gaelic oral tradition, devotion to a cult is not a requirement for a contemporary artist to use, and to preserve, the styles of the Afro-American oral tradition. Instead of dismissing this tradition as a pile of backward mumbo jumbo, perhaps we can learn through it to tolerate cultures that are different from our own, and maybe this knowledge will help us solve some of the complex problems that face our world.

Steven Spielberg Plays Howard Beach

*A*n audience of white and Asian feminists attending a rape-awareness workshop held in Berkeley last October said that they imagined the "stereotypical" rapist as black, until they were informed by Sallie Werson, a women's center counselor, that seventy-five to eighty percent of rapists are white.

Like the black bear and the North American wolf, the black male in the United States has been the subject of dangerous myths that often, as in the case of the bear and the wolf, lead people to shoot first and ask questions later. No black man, whatever his class, is exempt from superstitions about black men, a situation that causes anxiety and that probably accounts for the fact that black men suffer disproportionately from cancer, strokes, heart attacks, and other stress-related illnesses, including suicide and murder, which are now being viewed in the same manner as disease epidemics.

My disagreement with some feminists and womanists is that they have, out of ignorance or by design, promoted such myths in the media, a situation that adds to the problems that black men face in everyday life.

In the film *The Color Purple*, directed and produced by white males, all of the myths that have been directed at black men since the Europeans entered Africa are joined. In this

/ 145

film, black men commit heinous crimes against women and children, and though defenders of Walker's book, upon which the movie was based, argue that these creations were merely one woman's story, critics in the media have used both the book and the movie as excuses to indict all black men. This is not Ms. Walker's fault; however some of her public statements, such as her description of black men as "evil," gleefully printed in the magazine section of the neoconservative *New York Times*, haven't helped.

Gloria Steinem, media-appointed high priest person of American feminism, set the tone for the current group libel campaign against black men when she said, in the June 2, 1982 issue of *Ms.*, that the characterizations of black men in Ms. Walker's book represented "truth-telling." Since then this "truth-telling" line has been picked up by other feminists, womanists, and their male allies: bimps and wimps. Most recently, in an interview with a deferential San Francisco feminist, Alice Walker said that she was trying to tell the truth (*San Francisco Bay Guardian*, 17 September 1986).

Television critics Siskel and Ebert, when reviewing the movie, said that it was about offenses that black men have committed against black women. (Would they impute the crime against women by Jason, the hero of the *Friday the 13th* series, or by Freddy, in the *Nightmare on Elm Street* series, to all white men?) They described Ms. Walker as a feminist, even though Ms. Walker calls herself a womanist so as to separate herself and her followers from white feminists like "feminist scholar" Deidre English and Gloria Steinem, who publish her articles. Apparently Siskel and Ebert received some irate mail, because the week following their review, they hit black men again, this time for their inability to take criticism, which, in my opinion, supports charges against the media made by its critics: Once you get hit by the imperial media, whether you're an individual or a group, it's very difficult, if not impossible, to set the record straight.

When an interviewer asked me on "The Today Show" in late March of 1986 about the movie *The Color Purple*, I said that my primary criticism dealt with how "critics in the media were using the behavior of the black male characters to indict all black men." I apparently offended some viewers by going on to compare the movie's images of black men with those of Jewish males as child molesters, muggers, and rapists of Aryan females. This remark was based upon research of German newspapers and films, used in my novel *Reckless Eyeballing*, the publication of which was the ostensible reason for my appearing on "The Today Show," though the novel was never mentioned.

As soon as the novel *Reckless Eyeballing* was published, it became, as one reviewer said, "a literary tornado." I was invited to appear on "Tony Brown's Journal." In order to balance the show, Tony Brown's staff invited some prominent black feminists and womanists, including Michele Wallace, to appear. All of them declined. I suggested Barbara Smith, whose anthologies include *Home Girls* and *All the Women Are White, All the Blacks Are Men, But Some of Us Are Brave*.

Although a few of our exchanges were testy, Ms. Smith, one of the ablest proponents of the black feminist point of view, and I ended the show on friendly terms and, in April, greeted each other cordially at Storyville, in New Orleans. The famous jazz club had been rented by the Before Columbus

Foundation for presentation of the American Book Awards. Ms. Smith accepted an award for *This Bridge Called My Back*, edited by Cherrie Moraga and Gloria Anzaldus, a book that shows my disagreements with feminists to be mild in comparison to those between white feminists and black feminists.

Some of Ms. Smith's "sisters" were not so friendly as Ms. Smith. A few responded to the exchange between Ms. Smith and me by suggesting that I represented black male writers who were envious of black feminist writers. Others dismissed me with feminist rhetoric in which "misogynist" was the frequent buzzword.

A radical Chicago newspaper, which has apparently decided that black lesbian feminists constitute the revolutionary vanguard, dismissed my criticisms of *The Color Purple* as those of a "bohemian intellectual." One writer, in the *Gay Community News*, said that the issues Ms. Smith and I discussed shouldn't be debated at all, a stance that reinforced an opinion I formed many years ago in New York's East Village that while most Afro-Americans support democratic values, many black intellectuals yearn for the kind of one-party police states, operating in the rest of the world, where debate is stifled.

When I appeared as a member of a panel on the "Essence" television show in July, a new attack was raised by Max Robinson, the moderator: I was doing the same thing that I was accusing the black feminists of doing. This line was picked up by Richard Wesley, writing in the August issue of Gloria Steinem's *Ms.* magazine. (As an example of how *Ms.* magazine feminists treat even the black men who support their arguments, the editors at *Ms.* diminished the thrust of Mr. Wesley's article, which sought to disassociate Ms. Walker from the film *The Color Purple*, by attaching a footnote to the piece that revealed that Ms. Walker was the movie's consultant from the commencement of photography to the final cut.)

Though Mr. Wesley, author of the screenplay of Richard Wright's *Native Son*, suggested that there might be a "Literary Tribunal" for my "literary transgressions," neither Mr. Wesley nor Mr. Robinson could point to a single passage in my books in which a black woman rapes, pimps, or sells her children, nor will they find in my nonfictional writings a passage that says that such behavior is typical of black women.

The feminists who prompted Mr. Robinson and Mr. Wesley are sore with me because I included a mammy in my novel *Flight to Canada* (1976). They claim that such a character did not exist, when mammies appeared wherever colonialists settled. In the South, black women took care of white children; in Ireland, Irishwomen nurtured Anglo children; in Hawaii, Hawaiian women looked after the invader's children. These feminists, like zealots and ideologues everywhere, desire to rearrange history so that it includes only the parts supporting their feminist arguments and leaves out the parts that don't.

They've been on my case since my 1974 novel *The Last Days of Louisiana Red*, because it includes a feminist radical whose speeches they disapprove of. They complain about Tremonisha Smarts, of *Reckless Eyeballing*, because toward the end of the novel she leaves New York for California to have babies and to "write, write, write," which isn't inconsistent with the announced goal of a new generation of feminists: to have it all, a career and a family.

Some objected to the character's having children at all, because they are soured on reproduction. A group of storm-trooper California feminists booed poet Quincy Troupe because he read a poem about his child. One gains the impression that many feminists and womanists would like to do away with men altogether and turn the world into a sort of postgraduate seminar on feminism.

Though the "Essence" panel covered a number of issues over a two-hour period, the program was edited so that it came across as a tribute to Alice Walker, with me as some sort of crank, or cad.

Panelist Amiri Baraka praised Steven Spielberg, whose racism has been cited by Asian American organizations and most recently by an Irish American writer, Jack Foley, who, writing in the December 21 issue of *The San Jose Mercury*, complained about the images of Irish Americans in Spielberg's *An American Tail*. Mr. Baraka said that the right wing was offended by the film because the film exposed racism, which must come as news to Ronald and Nancy Reagan, who told a pre–Academy Awards show in 1986 that they enjoyed the film. Ms. Bush, the vice president's wife, attended a New York reception for the film; last I heard, the Reagans and the Bushes belonged to the political right wing.

On October 21, in the course of a hostile review of William Demby's *Love Story Black*, a novel that Steve Cannon and I published in 1978 and sold to E.P. Dutton in 1985, I was subjected to what might be called a drive-by literary shooting, when Greg Tate, writing in the *Village Voice*, remarked that I had "bitchy" attitudes toward "aggressive black women."

I have noticed that, in recent years, the *Voice* has printed lengthy articles regarding black male chauvinism, but I have never seen an article about the chauvinism of Italian American, Irish American, or Jewish American males, many of whom, according to the December 6, 1982 *New York Times*, engage in wife beating. Nor have I ever seen an article about women beating and abusing other women, which, according to a book entitled *Naming the Violence: Speaking Out About Lesbian Battering*, edited by Kerry Lobel, is a big problem.

Ms. magazine has also been relentless in its denouncement of black males, providing Alice Walker with the space to answer her critics in every issue, so it seems.

If the *Voice* and *Ms.* magazine are so concerned with the condition of black women, then why aren't any employed in the top staff or corporate positions? What are the attitudes of both publications toward "aggressive black women"? Rather than respond to Mr. Tate by engaging in the kind of blood-letting that occurs in the *Village Voice* letters column, on November 1, 1986, I sent out a press release challenging the *Voice* and *Ms.* to express their concerns for "aggressive black women" by hiring some of them for top positions on both publications. I added that, between I. Reed Books and Quilt anthology, as well as a number of other anthologies I've published since 1972, I've published more black women than both the *Voice* and *Ms.* combined. (I was the first to publish the fiction of a brilliant young writer named Michele Wallace.) Black women occupy, or have occupied, key positions in the Before Columbus Foundation, which I founded in 1976, and in There City Cinema, a foundation that I launched in 1985 to bring multicultural films to Oakland, California, for exhibit at a new cinema being built for the foundation by the City of Oakland.

By contrast the board of directors of the *Voice* are male, as are the publisher and the owner, a man who supports Mayor Koch, whose inflammatory racist rhetoric is partially responsible for the climate of racist terror that is now afflicting New York blacks. The top executive positions at *Ms.* as well as the important staff positions belong to white feminists.

I also said in the press release that the black women writers I publish write about a variety of subjects and are not just used to midwife the ideas of *Village Voice* feminists, who seem to be obsessed with black chauvinism. Gloria Steinem is not alone. It has been my experience that the most passionate defenders of the images of black males depicted in books and motion pictures like *The Color Purple*, and their clones, are white feminists.

I responded to a feminist scholar who asked me a belligerent question after I'd read a paper at the English Institute at Harvard last year by asking her why white feminists were so concerned about black male chauvinism yet seldom criticized the men of their own ethnic groups? She couldn't answer the question. Steven Spielberg said that *The Color Purple*, known in the book trade as a "bodice ripper," attracted a mostly white feminist audience, and with the movie he wanted to expand the audience.

I sent a copy of the press release to black writers at the *Voice*, whose brilliant prose is the main reason that I buy the newspaper. I also sent a copy to M. Mark, the feminist who edits the *Voice's* book review.

On November 19, black newspapers, including the *California Sun Reporter*, printed my release. I sent copies of the article to the same *Voice* staff members.

Newsweek, 1 December 1986, carried an article on blacks in journalism that included a passage that made a similar criticism of the *Village Voice*, which it described as a bastion of New York liberalism, at which only one of sixteen editors and one of nineteen staff writers are black. (*Newsweek* was wrong about there being a black senior editor at the *Voice*; there is none.)

On December 9, 1986, the head "Ishmael Reed's Female Troubles," introducing a "book review" written by Michele Wallace, appeared on the cover of the *Village Voice*. I think that the article was designed to make me feel bad, because it contained a number of unfriendly remarks, many of them erroneous, about my writings, about my career, and about me. I found it odd that Ms. Wallace, who has expressed her disdain for "patriarchy" in article after article, used the critical tools based upon the ideas of one of the most notorious and misogynistic of patriarchs, Sigmund Freud, to discuss my "perverse misogyny." Here was a man who concealed the fact that his friends were seducing their daughters (certainly a film project for Steven Spielberg). Also, for someone attempting to explain my ideas about "neo-HooDooism" to the *Voice*'s readership, Ms. Wallace spent a lot of time "psychoanalyzing" the image of the serpent in my novel *Reckless Eyeballing* without so much as a reference to the fact that the serpent is at the heart of Vodoun, a neo-African religion, upon which "neo-HooDooism" is based.

It seems that womanists who, among them, probably have over one hundred years of graduate school never question the theories pushed by the white male patriarchy. Maybe that's the reason that Ms. Wallace writes that womanists "leave the theorizing to others." I'm hip. This lack of a theory perhaps accounts for the erratic shifts in their concerns.

In a previous article, also printed in the *Village Voice*, during a discussion of Celie and Shug's idealized lesbian relationship, Ms. Wallace wrote that womanism was about achieving clitoral orgasm, yet in the *Voice* article about "Ishmael Reed's Female Troubles," she says that womanism is about poor, single black women and their children. There is no evidence that black men are better off than black women; in fact, one could say that womanists of Ms. Wallace's class are better off than black males of the same class.

The womanists also lack credibility when they complain about their "double oppression" and "other than otherness," when most of them are college professors or successful intellectuals who are better off than millions of destitute Americans, male and female, black and white. (This bickering among the "oppressed" over who is the most "oppressed" reminds me of the conflicts between German Jews and Eastern European Jews; when the Nazis rounded up the Jews, both groups went to the concentration camps.)

Ms. Wallace also errs when she describes such literary forms as the epic as white male inventions. The epic originated in Africa, and the novel form itself was created by Cervantes, a Moor.

The most significant error in the piece, I think, provides evidence for my chief complaint and disagreement with the feminists: their tendency to ascribe criminal sexual offenses committed against women and children by some black men to the majority of or to all black men, which is the kind of propaganda spread by the Ku Klux Klan and the American Nazi party. Citing my remark made on "Tony Brown's Journal" that Justice Department figures, released in July of 1985, attributed eighty percent of the sexual offenses to white males, Ms. Wallace writes that the actual number of sexual offenses committed by white males is fifty-two percent annually, a figure that not only makes no sense but implies that black males commit forty-eight percent of sexual offenses annually. (Another prominent feminist, during a television discussion with me, charged black men, as a group, with child molestation. Though no one denies that such practices exist, the typical child molester is a white, middle-class male, and his victim is a *boy*, but, when, during a television exchange with two feminists, I cited statistics, which were introduced at the 1986 Second National Conference on Social Structure, stating that fifty-two percent of the victims of female murderers were black men, I was confronted with the emotional outburst and performance art of debating strategies.*)

If Ms. Wallace's article was a reply to my press release questioning the *Voice*'s and *Ms.* magazine's attitudes toward "aggressive black women," then it's not sufficient. Until more black women are hired for the upper-echelon staff and policy-making positions, then one has to view their publications' obsessive concern for black women as insincere.

The discussion about the movie *The Color Purple* took a strange turn when it was revealed that Jon Lester, the teenager who led a lynch mob against three black men at Howard Beach in Queens, had seen the film *The Color Purple* and was described by a black girlfriend as being "real emotional" about it.

Jack Beatty, writing in the *New York Times* on January 7, cited this as evidence that Lester sympathized with the plight

---

*According to Nicholas Davidson, editor of *Gender Issues*, more women than men physically assault their spouses. Boys are as likely as girls to be victims of sexual abuse. A study of convicted rapists in California (Petrovich and Templer, 1984) discovered that nearly sixty percent had been abused as children by women. Most child abuse occurs in female-headed households.

of black people, and that his murderous actions were based upon some "territorial instinct," which is "also part of us." Mr. Beatty, whose magazine the *Atlantic Monthly* spent two issues in 1986 blaming poverty in America on "promiscuous" black women, described *The Color Purple* as "a story of a black woman's ordeal in the Jim Crow South," an odd interpretation, since many critics felt that the Jim Crow part was left out in favor of attributing the black women's ordeal, in the film, to malicious or, as Alice Walker would say, "evil" black men.

It is possible that Mr. Lester's lawyers might even use a *Color Purple* defense. They could argue, based upon his "emotional" reaction to the film, that the kid really loves black people but had drunk so much Southern Comfort that he couldn't think and that his "territorial instinct" took over; or they could plead insanity and say that he went crazy and thought of himself as "Indiana Jones," saving the Celies of this world.

Steven Spielberg said that when he read the book *The Color Purple*, all that he could think of was rescuing Celie. James Yee, one of Spielberg's Chinese American critics, charged that the movie *Indiana Jones and the Temple of Doom* was about Indiana Jones as "a white savior who rescues hordes of helpless Indian women and children from enslavement at the hands of *evil* Indian men" (my italics). (Ms. Wallace and her womanist clique will have to answer to history regarding the fact that they took a book about black male misogyny to Steven Spielberg, a man whose misogyny has been cited by a number of feminist critics, including Amy Taubin in the *Village Voice*. Does this mean that they'll let any male chauvinist who gives them some cash off the hook? Also, what would be the response if racist Bull Conner produced *The Martin Luther King Story* or Yasser Arafat, an anti-Semite, *Exodus?*)

Gloria Steinem, Steven Spielberg, Siskel and Ebert, and all of the others who've libeled black men could be called to testify on behalf of Mr. Lester, who no doubt will get his face on the 1980s yuppies, neoconservative Mount Rushmore.

I hope that the Howard Beach tragedy will persuade black feminists and womanists to understand that the criticisms of such films as *The Color Purple* (which made over $100 million, more than the annual revenues of many smokestack industries!) are not always based upon "envy" or spite but, just maybe, a justifiable paranoia. Film and television, besides being sources of entertainment, are the most powerful instruments of propaganda ever created by man, and the Nazi period has proved that, in sinister hands, they can be used to harm unpopular groups and scapegoats. (On television, black men are typically shown naked from the waist up, handcuffed, and leaning over a police car.)

A conversation I had with Ed Bullins, standing in a Berkeley bank a few weeks ago, sums it up. We decided that it could have been us, stranded in Howard Beach with a disabled car.

August Wilson: The Dramatist as Bearer of Tradition

One of the first black playwrights, Victor Sejour, wrote for white audiences. Born on June 2, 1821, in New Orleans, Sejour wrote twenty-one plays. *Diegansas*, his first play, was produced in 1844 at the Theatre Français in Paris. Since Sejour's time, many Afro-American playwrights have written plays that have enjoyed success with white audiences, but more than one black critic has attributed their success to the timidity of their forms and their content. One attracts mainstream audiences, they say, by mimicking European styles, and by diluting those that are uniquely Afro-American. Some of the Black Power playwrights of the 1960s and 1970s knew their Chekov and Beckett before they knew their Malcolm X.

For August Wilson, it was the other way around. The dramatic skills that Wilson has developed came after his conversion to the Black Power philosophies of Malcolm X and racial chauvinist Marcus Garvey and are mainly used to support his vision. He describes his theatrical aim as that of convincing his audience that Afro-Americans are an African people. His career is therefore paradoxical. As a playwright, August Wilson promotes black separatism, yet his audiences are "mainstream" audiences. Moreover, he has reached his audience without sacrificing the integrity of his plays' black styles. Just as the previously shunned black rock and roll can now be heard on the soundtrack of automobile commercials, August Wilson's acceptance may mean that the once-feared Black Power style of the 1960s has entered the mainstream, which is where many radical cultural movements have eventually settled.

As a student of the ironies of American civilization, I decided to explore the August Wilson phenomenon. I didn't see *Ma Rainey's Black Bottom*, because I was misled by the publicity. I prejudged it as merely one of a long series of "mammery" entertainments of the kind that have delighted and comforted white Americans since the days of Aunt Jemima and Hattie MacDaniel. After stopping off in New York on the way to New Haven to view the videotape of *Ma Rainey's Black Bottom*, through the courtesy of the Lincoln Center Film Library for the Performing Arts, I discovered my prejudices to be unfounded. Ma Rainey played only a minor role in the Wilson play. *Ma Rainey's Black Bottom* was about the conflicts between four black men.

August Wilson sat across from me in a booth inside Kavanagh's, a dimly lit restaurant and bar located across the street from the Duncan Hotel in New Haven. Soft-spoken to the point of inaudibility, hesitant, shy, an unfinished cheeseburger (cheddar) lying on his plate, he told me about his background and how he gained the support of Lloyd Richards, one of the most respected men in American theater. He wore a brown tweed jacket and bright red shirt open at the collar. Mr. Wilson is of medium height. His hairline is receding, but he radiates a fleshiness from his reddish face (though Mr. Wilson's avowed mission is that of portraying black Americans as an African people, his physical appearance suggests a European, Native

American—possibly Cherokee—as well as African background; he speculates that his father might have been white).
Maybe it was his beard and sensual eyes that convinced me
that you could take his head and torso and place them on the
lower parts of a horse, and you'd have a satyr in a Renaissance
painting. His new play, *Fences*, which was performed at the
Yale Repertory Theatre in May of 1985, was being prepared
for performances at Chicago's Goodman Theatre beginning
on February 10, a theater supported by subscribers. We met,
for the first time, on the day before a Sunday rehearsal that I
attended.

By the time I reached New Haven, I felt as though I had
navigated a maze: the phone calls made to Lincoln Center's
Film Library so I might view the videotape of Wilson's *Ma
Rainey's Black Bottom*; the additional phone calls to ascertain
the availability of August Wilson and Lloyd Richards for interviews. Getting into rehearsal was like arranging to view a
gem on loan from a private collection. None of this could
have been accomplished without the assistance of Judy Fish,
Lloyd Richards's assistant.

After talking to Wilson, I could understand why Richards
would desire to protect this talent that he says he serves. August
Wilson is more than a playwright; he's what some Native
American scholars would call a "tradition-bearer," one who
knows the old stories and reveres the precise styles in which
they are rendered. You don't learn that in school, and so
though Wilson's official education ended in the ninth grade,
his other education took place in those academies of the Afro-
American literary oral tradition: the street corners (Fullerton
and Wylie streets in Pittsburgh, called by Harlem Renaissance
author Claude McKay "the crossroads of the world"); the res-

taurants, and the gambling dens. Places like Pittsburgh's Eddie's Restaurant on Centre Avenue. Sefu's Place and Pat's Place. Places where the old-timers gathered to play the dozens, signify, and indulge in other hyperbolic word games. Ever the good listener (I asked him the origin of the line, "You're a day late and a dollar short" that appears in *Fences*; he said he got it from his mother), his job as a cook and dishwasher gave him a front-row-center seat for this rich verbal entertainment and instruction; these occupations also account for the accurate descriptions of soul food that appear in his work. It was in Pittsburgh, from 1965 to 1968, that Wilson came in contact with other black writers at the Centre Avenue Poet's Theatre Workshop, and the Half Way Art Gallery, which was financed by Saint Stephen's Church. Some of those writers have gone to the penitentiary, and into drugs, but Wilson has survived. He is a survivor. His most frequently used expression is "life-force."

In the 1960s, Wilson came under the influence of Black Power philosophies and credits them with having shaped his political opinions. Both of the writers he mentions as his influences returned to the universities some time ago. One recently admitted that he invented a black Christmas holiday that was formerly thought to have originated in East Africa; and though the famous principles of his "Black Value System" were not meant for outsiders, I heard them recited by a group of white, black, Asian, and Hispanic children during a program at Berkeley's Le Conte School and found them to be "universal." The other writer mentioned as one of Wilson's chief influences recently published an autobiography in which he confesses that after a trip to Africa he realized that he was an

American after all. So is Wilson, and though he may argue that blacks and whites are different, or have his characters dare "the white man's God," Wilson's ideas would find no disagreement from some of America's fundamentalist TV evangelists; for example, his comment that God does not hear the prayers of blacks. Apple-pie virtues such as self-reliance and the family are among the major concerns of his plays.

It was Charles Davis, the late Yale professor, who, in his book *Black Is the Color of the Cosmos*, pointed out that the 1960s Black Power philosophies were in the American tradition. Unlike some of our armchair neoconservative philosophers, Wilson's notions about the family and self-reliance have been verified by his experience. He discovered when he lived in Pittsburgh's Arlington Heights projects in 1972 and 1973 that only 17 out of 604 units contained families that were headed by a male, but on weekends the parking lots would be full.

Wilson believes that a man should have responsibility for his family. Again, in *Fences*, Troy Maxson, though flawed by corruption, arrogance, and though a man of limited vision and a convicted felon (he robbed to feed his family), never abandons his family.

I asked Wilson why his *Fences* character, Alberta, didn't obtain an abortion; he said that "the seed shouldn't be squandered," revealing, perhaps, his Roman Catholic background.

Wilson's characters are types. Some are after good times, like the womanizer, Slow Drag, and Dussie Mae in *Ma Rainey*, who uses sex to obtain favors from both men and women. Others are saintly. Like Ruth in *A Raisin in the Sun* (directed by Lloyd Richards in 1958), Rose in *Fences* holds the family together even if it means taking in her husband's child by another woman (I told Wilson that I thought that this was stretching it).

Others have great talents that are stunted by a racist society. Ma Rainey insists that she is the "mother of the blues," and acts like it, ordering her producers and agent about, scolding her musicians, and in one scene costing her producer money ("Damn the cost," she says) by insisting that her nephew, a stutterer, introduce a new song. The producer fumes while the stutterer does a number of takes until he gets it right. Yet despite her boldness, Ma Rainey is as economically exploited as her musicians, who are paid the same amount of money, twenty-five dollars, as her nephew. After prison, Troy Maxson plays baseball, but even though he hits seven home runs off Satchel Paige, his career is stifled by racism; Troy says, "I just wasn't the right color."

In Wilson's plays, men of the clergy, athletes, and blues singers are as much affected by the evils of racism as are common people, and just because a black person becomes famous doesn't guarantee that he will have economic security. Troy doesn't want his son, Cory, to play football but to study. He doesn't want the son to be disillusioned as he was. In one scene he tells his wife, Rose, who can't understand his decision to prohibit his son from playing football: "I saw Josh Gibson's daughter yesterday. She walking around with raggedy shoes on her feet." And for every black achiever there are hundreds with the same ability who are denied the opportunity to use their talents because of racism. Troy says: "I done seen a hundred niggers play baseball better than Jackie Robinson. Hell, I know some teams Jackie Robinson couldn't even make."

Wilson writes about the black lower middle class, those

wedged between poverty and the middle class. Their values are conservative, and their faith in the American Dream unwavering. They know that only through luck, the lottery, numbers (what Richards calls "the one shot"), or an unexpected contract (contracts offer a way out in Wilson's plays, just as their father's money rescued Walter Lee's family in A *Raisin in the Sun*) will they be able to rise above their station. Maybe they won't make it, but their children will. And so they place their hopes on the next generation. At the end of *Fences*, all of the characters who remain after Troy's death, according to Wilson, are institutionalized except Troy's child, Raynell. For August Wilson, she represents the Afro-American future, just as Lorraine Hansberry's remarkable Beneatha is the forerunner of the black feminist movement.

Not only are Wilson's characters victims of their times' racism, they are heirs to the disaster that occurred during the nineteenth century when whatever gains blacks made during the reconstruction period were forfeited through back contracts and mob violence. As their game of the dozens (complicated and sometimes vicious—the dozens in *Ma Rainey* end with a death—wordplay of an insulting nature that uses hyperbole and humor to make points) heats up, Toledo, the cynical intellectual in *Ma Rainey*, accuses the character Levee of being spooked by the white man, whereupon Levee tells the story of his father, an "uppity" nigger who owned fifty acres of good farming land in Jefferson County about eighty miles outside of Natchez, Mississippi. Envious, eight or nine white men raped his mother while his father was in flight from them. Levee suffered a knife wound while attempting to protect his mother. Before he was lynched, Levee's father slew four of his wife's attackers. Similarly, Troy's father, a sharecropper, was so indebted to the landlord, Mr. Lubin, that he lived his life as a packhorse, frustrated and "evil." Though he remained with his family, as Troy does, he abused them for the misery of his life. Wilson, in his poetic introduction to *Fences*, expresses his belief that white Europeans had an easier time blending into American society than did blacks, and that the nineteenth century and early twentieth century were key periods during which the arriving immigrants began their slow but relentless move from Ellis Island to the suburbs. While the first generation of white immigrants began to accumulate the assets that would be passed on to succeeding generations, the parallel black generation was being robbed. (At one point Wilson said, "I write for my grandfather.") What happened to Levee and Troy's father was typical as blacks were excluded from the country's economic and political life.

Blacks did not begin to recover from these and similar disasters until the late 1950s, the period covered in *Fences*.

August Wilson is faithful to the values of the class he writes about, values familiar to me, to Richards, and possibly to James Earl Jones, some of whose autobiographical details jibe with those of Wilson and Richards. Before the rise of the civil rights movement, individual resistance to racism occurred in everyday life. Troy complains about the sanitation department he works for leaving all the dirty work to the blacks while the whites drive the trucks. "You think only white fellows got sense enough to drive a truck. That ain't no paper job! Hell, anybody can drive a truck." My mother during the same 1950s demanded from her employers an explanation as to why the white girls worked the cash register and the black girls had to do stock work. "I have a high school education," she said, and she was promoted. For the black lower middle class, nothing comes easy, and like members of this class, August Wilson has earned his niche as one of the United States' most gifted playwrights, undergoing an arduous apprenticeship (*Ma Rainey* and *Fences* were rewritten a number of times), braving setbacks and disappointment, and living in poverty. (Five years ago he married June Oliver, a Minnesota social worker.) It didn't come easy.

His first theatrical efforts were staged by the Black Horizon Theatre, a group he helped to organize in 1968 to, in the language of the times, "raise the consciousness of the community." He couldn't write dialogue, an art that he began developing after he moved to Saint Paul, Minnesota, but he rated his descriptive powers as good. In 1977, a friend, Claude Purdy, suggested that Wilson turn a series of poems into a play. The result was Wilson's *Black Bart and the Sacred Hills*, which was "inspired by you" he said to me, the interviewer (I was the author of a poem entitled "Badman of the Guest Professor," which includes an allusion to Black Bart, the stagecoach robber and poet who gave Wells Fargo some problems in the 1870s). *Black Bart*, a musical satire, was produced in 1978 at the Penumbra Theatre after Wilson moved to Saint Paul in March of that year. He got a job in the Science Museum of Minnesota, writing scripts for a theater troupe. The hindrance to his writing dialogue, he decided, was his tendency to use the characters to recite his poetry instead of making them distinct. He also credits the move from Pittsburgh for developing his skills at writing dialogue. *Black Bart* was well received, but in hindsight, Wilson feels that the play's twenty-seven characters made it unwieldy.

The theme of self-reliance was taken up in his second play, *Jitney*, about a group of black gypsy-cab drivers who organize their own company, foreshadowing the ambitions of Levee, the character in *Ma Rainey* who desires to form his own band. *Jitney* was given a reading in 1980 and was produced in Pittsburgh in 1982. After receiving a Jerome Fellowship for *Jitney* in June of 1980, Wilson began to think of himself as a playwright. He heard about the Eugene O'Neill Conference, and in 1980 sent *Black Bart and the Sacred Hills*, *Fullerton Street*, a play set in the 1940s (it's Wilson's announced intention to write a play about the struggle of blacks during each decade of the twentieth century), and *Why I Learned to Read*, about two black teenagers who choose safer careers after a robbery attempt fails. It was after these plays were rejected that Wilson began to apply his steadily improving skills to the play that, according to one writer, "catapulted Wilson to the forefront of young American playwrights": *Ma Rainey's Black Bottom*.

Wilson, who was born in Pittsburgh on April 27, 1945, first heard Bessie Smith when he was twenty years old. "It was the first time someone was speaking directly to me," he remembers of the experience. Bessie Smith, who was given her first break by Ma Rainey, led Wilson to Ma Rainey, Victoria Spivey, and other blues singers. And so it was these blues records that sold for five cents apiece at the St. Vincent De Paul's Pittsburgh store that inspired Wilson's blues and dozens play about economic exploitation, dashed hopes, and desperations—themes which Langston Hughes captured in his moving lines "What happens to a dream deferred? / Does it dry up / like a raisin in the sun?" (Lloyd Richards eloquently calls this condition "the deprivation of possibility.")

Wilson had read Hughes and other Harlem Renaissance writers in the libraries of Pittsburgh. In the first version of *Ma Rainey*, written in 1976, the year during which a rash of plays about black women began to appear, Ma Rainey was the principal character, and Dussie Mae, her lover, had more lines than in the final version produced at Yale and in New York. The musicians were present only to accompany her. The idea to develop the four musicians occurred to Wilson while he was reading a draft of the play. From that experience came Levee, Slow Drag, and Toledo, all of whose names have allegorical significance, except for Cutler, who was named for Wilson's grandfather.

Wilson submitted *Ma Rainey's Black Bottom* to the Eugene O'Neill Conference in 1982; the thirty-six-page play was selected for workshops and readings. This brought Wilson in contact with Lloyd Richards, the man who would give Wilson's vision technical depth and range. Wilson is deliberately naive about the theater. He doesn't read or attend plays. When he wrote poetry, he feels that he was an imitator because he read the masters. Wilson wants his own style.

The night before I interviewed Richards, I ran into him at one of the sixth annual Winterfest parties that was held at the Yale Repertory's home, a former church purchased by Yale in the 1960s. He seemed to be very officious. He was doing his fund-raising chores, I was told. The youthful party crowd was well scrubbed and prosperous. The son of a famous movie mogul was pointed out to me as he dipped into the punch bowl. Besides fund-raising, Richards, as dean of the Yale Drama School, teaches classes and administers the Yale Repertory Theatre's three million dollar budget.

He also directs the annual National Playwright Conference at the Eugene O'Neill Memorial Theatre Center in Waterford, where he reads sixty to seventy plays per year and works seven days a week, days which according to Richards have no limits.

He is a member of the playwrights selection committee of the Rockefeller Foundation as well, and in March of 1975 he was appointed by President Reagan to a seat on the National Council for the Arts. A busy man whose job is mostly nondirecting, he prefers working at Yale to working in the commercial theater, where "one does what is available, instead of what one wants to do." For Richards, the structure that runs the theater world is a hierarchy, and those projects the people at the top discard trickle down to the lower echelons. He refers to Broadway as "the theater industry" where "hits" and "blockbusters" appeal to "the plastic card crowd."

Lloyd Richards is almost religiously (he was once a lay reader in the Episcopal Church) devoted to the theater. He desires to devote his life to molding new directors, actors, set designers, stage managers, and composers. Yale Repertory Theatre provides students with the rare opportunity to participate in Broadway and regional theater productions; Yale students played key roles in the production of *Ma Rainey's Black Bottom*. When Richards speaks about the theater he loses his stiffness, and his eyes shine. Theater will survive, Richards believes, because unlike television and film it can bring live performers before a live audience, and each performance is unique. In the theater, Richards believes, one is in "communion" with the people on stage and in the audience. Richards is obviously enjoying himself as Yale Repertory's "Artistic Director," a title he says doesn't reflect the magnitude of the job—but life wasn't always so rewarding.

The hurt is still in his eyes if you search closely enough. His eyes are the instruments he uses to express anger and annoyance as well as euphoria, as when James Earl Jones, playing Troy during rehearsal, was performing brilliantly and getting off some pointed and sharp lines to Cory, his son. His voice is invariably pleasant even when he is reprimanding one of his assistants during rehearsal: "I've been here for over an hour and you haven't offered me coffee, tea, or anything," he said, in a voice dipped in honey, but firm.

I asked him about "archetypes," one of Wilson's favorite words that appears in both *A Raisin in the Sun* and Wilson's plays. Walter Lee, Levee, and Troy are similarly, in Wilson's words, "strong and spirited," tormented men pacing up and down like lions, raging at the demons of racism; Ruth and Rose, the dutiful wives who hold the family together, Mama, in *Raisin*, and Ma Rainey shrewd, tough, and domineering women. I wondered did some of the situations in Hansberry's and Wilson's plays coincide with situations in Richards's background? Was this what Richards meant when he said, after reading Wilson's plays, "I knew those characters"? Wilson never knew his father, and Richards's father died when he was nine. Before Hansberry's Mama and Wilson's Ma there was Richards's mother, Rose, holding the family together after his father's death. "She would even call up the mayor," Wilson said, chuckling with pride. In the 1920s, the Richards family migrated from Canada to Detroit in order to take advantage of Henry Ford's five-dollar-per-day labor incentive. Like Wilson, Richards was acquainted with the unofficial academies of the Afro-American oral tradition. He worked in barbershops and shined shoes where noisy jukeboxes would never intrude and the chief recreation was storytelling, playing the dozens, and signifying. Richards was introduced to *Macbeth* in grade school, a play that obviously made an impression on him. Though at one time he contemplated becoming a lawyer, it is the theater that has held his heart.

When August Wilson's work was introduced to Richards, Wilson was a poet in the process of becoming a playwright. I had noticed that the script for *Ma Rainey* contained few directions. It was Richards who designed the play's choreography. While watching the videotape of the play, I was struck by how the music that introduces some of the scenes sets the play's mood. This was also Richards's decision. When Wilson does something that very few playwrights would attempt, Richards does not change the script but works around it. Richards had to solve the problem of casting the four major musicians who appear in *Ma Rainey*. Should he cast actors or musicians? He cast actors who spent time with brilliant young Yale composer Dwight Andrews learning how to play musical instruments. Both live music and taped music performed by professional musicians were used during the performances. It was tricky, Richards said. The album made from *Ma Rainey's Black Bottom* recently won a Grammy.

The idea to use a two-tiered stage was also Richards's, "so that the action could flow," he explained. Richards sees his job as that of serving the playwright's intent. Intent is the key word that describes his directorial approach. He says that he uses whatever talents he has to support, extend, supplement the playwright's intent. He does not wish to "impose upon a work," but to "illuminate it." Wilson gets away with ideas that some would consider hokey. Imagine someone in this day and age ending a play with the characters staring off into the sunset, as Gabriel, Troy's demented brother—he wears a plate as the result of a war injury—plays the trumpet for Troy's journey to heaven. But didn't they say that abstract expressionism would finish off realists like Grant Wood? Grant Wood has made a strong comeback. Maybe Wilson is right.

When Wilson's *Ma Rainey* arrived at the Eugene O'Neill Conference, some thought that the play was actually two plays, but after the rewrites and the workshops, *Ma Rainey* became one play. As director of the O'Neill, Richards cannot express favoritism toward a project until the conference concludes. A producer was interested in *Ma Rainey*, but six months later the deal fell through. It was then that Wilson informed Richards of the play's availability.

On April 6, 1984, *Ma Rainey's Black Bottom* opened at the Yale Repertory Theatre to critical praise. Frank Rich of the *New York Times* heralded Richards as a major find for the American theater. On October 11, 1984 the play opened at the Cort Theatre on Broadway, where it was also well received by critics. In May of 1985, the Yale Repertory Theatre produced *Fences*.

On Saturday at 11:30 AM I followed Richards into the Colony Inn, where I was to interview him. I could see him scanning the room for my presence; he turned around and I was standing there. He is five feet four inches tall, stocky in a compressed sort of way, and wears a grayish white beard; his hair is the same color. His glasses are of an austere style, and he dresses with Prussian meticulousness, navy blue sweater, brilliant white shirt, and green tie. Though he has an aristocratic bearing, he could probably give a good account of himself in a street fight. While growing up innocent in Buffalo, we'd heard of places like Detroit and Philadelphia, where people robbed you at gunpoint while you were waiting for the traffic light to change, or where teenagers were supposed to have entered parties shooting. I told Richards that while living on New York's Lower East Side during my early twenties, I dated a hip NYU art history major and visited her in his apartment on Washington Square while she babysat for his family. I didn't tell him that, at the time, I thought the place to be the epitome of bourgeois comfort; in those days I thought that there was some connection between creative talent and penury.

At one o'clock we entered the Afro-American Cultural Center on York Street where rehearsals for the play were taking place. Ray Aranha, Mary Alice, Charles Brown, Frankie Falson, Courtney B. Vance, the excellent cast, were already there. As the rehearsal unfolded, I could see that Lloyd Richards's well-known eye for detail (his favorite director is Akira Kurosawa) extends to the casting of a play, because the actors fit perfectly the characters they were playing.

Momentarily, James Earl Jones bounded in. He was dressed as Troy Maxson; he wore white sneakers, jeans, a safari-styled jacket with a dark brown patch above the right breast, a blue shirt open at the collar, and a blue baseball cap. He still has black eyebrows, mustache, but some gray has crept into his beard. His penetrating eyes, covered by big, round glasses, are set above prominent cheekbones. His forehead is square. He had apparently put on some weight in order to play Troy. I introduced myself, but he was testy and aloof. I didn't take it personally. I'd read his citation of Lee Strasberg when praising Lloyd Richards and interpreted his attitude as that of an actor getting to the insides of his character. During the break, he was quite friendly, with an ingratiating smile, as we discussed his now-famous feat of learning a new second act for Phillip Dean Hayes's *Paul Robeson* on the train between Philadelphia and Boston. This example of his professionalism and dedication occurred during performances for the first play that Richards and Jones collaborated on. Jones's famous deep and powerful voice shook the churchlike building where the rehearsal was taking place as he gave a brilliant portrayal of the play's tragic hero. Jones seemed at home with the material. His Michigan memories are similar to those of Wilson and Richards, for whom he once served as understudy in Elia Kazan's *The Egghead*.

In an interview printed in *Theatre*, a magazine published by the Yale School of Drama and the Yale Repertory Theatre, he said: "I can also relate to the oral tradition: my grandfather, my father, even my mother were always telling stories. That is a very African tradition. Dark people did not write it; it was passed on orally. That's very much a part of what I heard in the play."

I spent three and one-half hours watching the rehearsal, excusing myself for about fifteen minutes so that I could check out of the Duncan Hotel and not be charged for an additional day. (Hotel space was scarce because of the Winterfest activities. I thought I'd enhance my chances of obtaining a room there by mentioning to the reservations clerk that I was writing a magazine article about one of its illustrious guests. "We don't need publicity. We've been here for ninety-two years," the person on the other end of the line said, with all the charm of the caretaker in the horror movie *The Haunting*, which must have been about New England. Nevertheless, the management was able to book me into a huge room on the seventh floor.)

During the rehearsal, Richards sat as sombre as a federal judge between Terry Witter, assistant stage manager, and stage manager Joel Drummond. Richards took the cast through a number of takes of act 2 of the two-act play. He never raised his voice and occasionally looked over his shoulder at me, the intruder, which is what I felt like. I glanced at a sheet of notes lying on the table in front of one of Richards's assistants. It read VISITOR TODAY.

A platform with three steps leading to it represented the stage. A red stool had been placed in front of the platform. Throughout the rehearsal, balloons left over from the Winterfest party held the night before descended to the floor. A thunderstorm served as the perfect accompaniment to Jones's resonant speeches. He had become the fifty-three-year-old baseball player, Troy, dreaming about another chance, only to be denounced by his wife for having a baby by Alberta, the other woman. (I asked Richards why there wasn't a liberated woman in *Fences*, as there was in *Ma Rainey* and *Raisin*. He said that Alberta was liberated. The answer puzzled me at first, but then I recalled that in the 1960s, liberated feminist intellectuals had urged women to have fatherless children.) I watched the cast execute a splendid performance, playing off Jones's energy as Troy, a man whose tragic flaw is his color and whose hubris occurs when he tries to, in Wilson's poetic metaphor, steal second base only to be tagged out by Death, which he tries to stave off with a fence. The mood in the rehearsal space was serious. Reverential. The actors and actresses obviously respected the material. They displayed the kind of earnestness that I noticed from some Irish American actors and actresses in a production of *The Iceman Cometh*, directed by Charles Gordone.

Richards's directions dealt mostly with movement. He repeatedly told Courtney B. Vance, the actor playing Cory, not to cross the line when his mother, Rose, played by Mary Alice, is talking about Troy's daughter, Raynell. Frankie Falson, who portrays Gabriel, was told to walk closer to a stage tree. Richards spent time instructing Cory on how to lift Rose, which happens in act 2, scene 4, when Cory arrives home from the marines on the day of Troy's funeral. "Don't lift her off the steps," Richards insisted.

He warned him about too many hugs that might appear to be "cloying." I began to understand why Richards referred to himself as a choreographer. Indeed the line between choreography and directing has always been blurred. The fight that takes place in act 2, scene 4, the play's most dramatic scene, was indeed choreographed by Richards. Cory challenges Troy's claim and his manhood by revealing that the house Troy bought, "my house," was actually paid for by Troy's brother Gabriel's money. Cory: "It ain't your yard! You took Uncle Gabe's money he got from the army to buy this house . . . then you put him out." Troy (advances on him): "You get your black ass out of my yard."

I wondered how James Earl Jones felt, his prodigious hulk sprawled on the floor while his fellow actors played the scene that occurs on the day of Troy's funeral. Wilson says that he created the character Troy with Jones in mind. Did Jones feel, as his character does, that racism had hampered his opportunity to display his formidable talents? Did Richards? Did Wilson? And if, as Wilson says, female-headed households are devolutionary situations—Lyons, Troy's first son, follows Troy's route to the penitentiary because he was raised by a woman, Troy's first wife, and not a man—then how does one account for the success of Richards and Wilson?

I pondered these questions as I left the playwright, director, and lead actor, who collaborate the way Duke Ellington, Billy Strayhorn, and Johnny Hodges must have collaborated.

Three incidents that took place before and after my trip to New Haven made me appreciate this collaboration even more.

Before I arrived in New Haven I sat in a World Literature class at a black university, and though the students were acquainted with the standard names included in such a course, they knew nothing of the storytelling forms that Wilson, Richards, and Jones know so well. Bruce Jackson, a Jewish American and one of the best scholars on the subject of the Afro-American literary oral tradition, says that the old forms are dying out, victims of assimilation. Some forms, like the Work Song, are extinct. The Thursday after I left Yale I was in Alaska, attending a publishing conference sponsored by the Native American Raven's Bones Foundation. Ronn E. Dick, a professor of Nature Resources at Sitka, Alaska's Sheldon Jackson College, during a panel lamented the passing of the Native American oral and dance traditions. He spoke of how the Cherokee Stomp Dance and the Sun Dance of the Sioux and Cheyenne had all but disappeared. The tragedy for him was that these traditions were used to impart lessons of morality and ethics to the young.

The didacticism and allegory carried in Wilson's work may seem square to the jaded critics of today, but these elements are mainstays in the Afro-American as well as the Native American oral and movement traditions. With the alarming statistics regarding unwed mothers—not just a black "problem," but a national one—crime, and other symptoms of what sociologists call "social anomie," perhaps didacticism is undergoing a revival.

The final incident occurred when my mother (who would be a part of Wilson's natural constituency) called to express her indignation about a Hollywood version of black life she'd just seen. "I never knew any blacks like those . . . and what's all of this about women kissing each other!" She and my stepfather rarely go to the theater, and when I took them to see a San Francisco production of Charles Fuller's *The Soldier's Story*, they sat, riveted and fascinated. They enjoyed this play, just as they would enjoy plays by Ed Bullins and August Wilson, playwrights who, in Wilson's words, "dig beneath the surface" of Afro-American culture. I thought of my mother, and the millions of hardworking blacks who are devoted to those traditional values that Wilson writes about, but who may never have the opportunity to see his work as long as profit is the motivating force behind Hollywood and the American commercial stage. The Broadway production of *Ma Rainey* lost money. As for Wilson, a hybrid both culturally and physically, despite his avowed blackness (he refers to himself as a "cultural nationalist," another term for ethnic chauvinism), he is bound to get even stronger as a playwright, under the tutelage of Lloyd Richards, of whose importance Ron Whyte wrote: "Richards's theater career marks him as one of the major forces of the American theater of the past three decades." Realism will not hold Wilson, and his future plays, *Joe Turner's Come and Gone*, and *The Piano Lesson*, promise to move more toward the unreal, the supernatural. *Joe Turner* will include ghosts, exorcism, and a root doctor; a piano will be the symbolic core of *The Piano Lesson*. These productions should be worth the wait.

Killer Illiteracy

I'm beginning to believe that Killer Illiteracy ought to rank near heart disease and cancer as one of the leading causes of death among Americans. What you don't know can indeed hurt you, and so those who can neither read nor write lead miserable lives, like Richard Wright's character, Bigger Thomas, born dead with no past or future. If they're hungry they don't know how to fill out an application for food stamps or, since much of the information about the world is shut off from them, may never have heard of the food stamp program. If they're injecting themselves with heroin, the favorite pastime of thousands of people in Northern California who have no better way to stimulate their imaginations, they don't know that dirty needles can give you AIDS, thereby threatening generations of the unborn with their ignorance.

If you're illiterate, people can do anything they want to you. Take your house through equity scams, cheat you, lie to you, bunko you, take your money, even take your life. Illiterate people get used in diabolical experiments such as the Tuskegee Program, in which unsuspecting black males were injected with syphilis by government Dr. Mengeles.

As you go through life X-ing documents, unable to defend yourself against forces hostile to you, people can deprive you of your voting rights through gerrymandering schemes, build a freeway next to your apartment building, or open a retail crack operation on your block, with people coming and going as though you lived next door to Burger King—because you're not articulate enough to fight back, because you don't have sense enough to know what is happening to you, and so you're shoveled under at each turn in your life; you might as well be dead.

One of the joys of reading is the ability to plug into the shared wisdom of mankind. One of my favorite passages from the Bible is "Come, and let us reason together"—Isaiah 1:18. Being illiterate means that you often resort to violence, during the most trivial dispute—the kind of disputes that would inspire hilarious skits on "Saturday Night Live" if they weren't so tragic—because you don't have the verbal skills to talk things out. I'm sure this is the reason why some "minority" males are participating in a mutual extermination to such an extent that the homicide statistics in "minority communities" read as though an Iran–Iraq war of fratricide was happening within our borders.

I'm also convinced that illiteracy is a factor contributing to suicide becoming one of the leading causes of death among white middle-class youngsters, who allow their souls to atrophy from the steady diet of spiritual Wonder Bread: bad music, and bad film, and the outrageous cheapness of superficial culture. When was the last time you saw a movie or TV program that was as good as the best book you've read, and I don't mean what imitation elitists call the classics. I'd settle for Truman Capote, John A. Williams, Cecil Brown, Lawson Inada, Paule Marshall, Xam Wilson Cartier, Victor Cruz, Howard Nemerov, William Kennedy, Paula Gunn Allen,

Margaret Atwood, Diane Johnson, Edward Field, Frank Chin, Rudolfo Anaya, Wesley Brown, Lucille Clifton, Al Young, Amiri Baraka, Simon Ortiz, Bob Callahan, Richard Grossinger, David Meltzer, Anna Castillo, Joyce Carol Thomas and Harryette Mullen, a group of writers as good as any you'd find anywhere, but who seldom make the curriculum of oil-money intellectuals like Alan Bloom, author of *The Closing of the American Mind.*

Bloom's love of the classics was revealed as phony by Martha Nussbaum in a devastating piece on this cultural Col. Blimp in the November 5 issue of the *New York Review of Books.* Bloom represents the kind of people who are driving students away from reading. The kind of people who fill our students with dead diction and archaic styles and perpetuate the idea that good writing can be found only in a seventeenth-century vault.

Illiteracy not only affects members of the "underclass" but reaches into the centers of higher education. It has been revealed that many of our college students have difficulty with even the bonehead level of English. To remedy this situation, AWP newsletter, a publication of the associated writing program, is urging that more professional writers, a sort of United States Writing Corps, be sent into our public schools and universities to acquaint students with writing as a useful tool, as well as something that enriches one's experience.

To say that the job should be left exclusively to critics and theorists is to say that a food critic knows as much about food as a chef, or that one can learn to build a cabinet by reading the history of furniture. AWP is also correct in its proposal that the hiring, rank, and tenure of teachers of writing "should be based on the quality of the individual's writing and teaching" and that "academic degrees should not be considered a requirement or a major criterion which would overrule the importance of the writer's achievement in the art." This proposal becomes more important when you learn that a poet of Philip Levine's stature was denied a teaching job at a local university because he lacked a Ph.D. These people who fill the curriculum with thousands of courses on Shakespeare would have denied Shakespeare a job because he lacked a degree.

One of the exercises I give when I visit Berkeley and Oakland schools involves having students write about their activities, from the time they rose in the morning until they arrived in school. This exercise not only gives me an opportunity to demonstrate how raw material, through skillful editing and revision, can be transformed into a polished manuscript, but how writing can involve normal conversational language, and that the techniques of fiction and poetry can be found in everyday language, and that writing can be fun, and not just a solemn visit to the cemetery, the opinion of the great mind who included in the Oakland high school equivalency test a question that only a specialist in middle English should be required to answer.

The person who designed this question perhaps thinks of himself as a traditionalist, who, like many traditionalists, desires to impose bigotry upon the "ancients," who were a cosmopolitan people, and would never put themselves in dumb antiintellectual positions like opposing ethnic or women's studies, or bilingual education, or trying to avoid linguistic change by making one language the official language of the state, a gesture as foolish as opposing a comet. How many of these traditionalists will admit that Terence, a Roman playwright, was black, or that a few of the early popes were black, or that if it weren't for Arab translators, they wouldn't even have access to the Great Books they're always pretending to love?

Left up to these geniuses we'd all be speaking Old Norse. There is a whole army of these types spread out across the country who are boring students into illiteracy, all because they're more interested in some kind of quixotic struggle in the name of a mythical tradition instead of being concerned about whether our students can read and write.

I studied, and enjoyed, white male literature for about the first 20 years of my life (the few women we read were tokens, like the Brontë sisters), but I really became interested in writing when I read James Baldwin and Richard Wright. They proved to me that a person of my background could write as well as the rest of them. You'd think that the modern curriculum would include books by Hispanics, Asian Americans, Afro-Americans—not just the token one or two who are there for the wrong reasons—so as to demonstrate to children of those cultures what persons of their backgrounds have accomplished.

Including multicultural literature in the curriculum would also acquaint students who are ignorant of other American cultures with the range of experience found within them. Certainly, if, according to Terry Eagleton, the turn-of-the-century goal of teaching literature was to create better men, then literature can also be used to promote understanding between groups, a job that's unfortunately left to TV and the movies, whose goal seems to be that of raising lynch mobs against minorities. I knew that my course in multicultural literature at Dartmouth was a success when a black student told me that after reading John Okada and Louis Chou, she'd discovered that Asian Americans weren't all the same, a lesson that our hysterical inflammatory news media, which are always lumping thirty-eight culturally distinct groups as one people, haven't learned.

Certainly, the monoculturalists and their allies who have such a powerful influence over the design of the school curricula must share some of the blame for the appalling rate of literacy in the United States, but parents who leave the job of teaching writing and reading to the schools must also bear some of the responsibility.

These parents don't have a book in the house, not even a newspaper that can be as instructive as any work of literature, because some of our finest writers have been newspaper people. James Reston, Robert Maynard, Brenda Payton, Warren Hinckle, Hunter Thompson are as good as any of the "major" writers now publishing in the United States. For parents to believe that the job should be left to teachers means that they haven't visited a classroom where one teacher is in charge of thirty students, and because of budget cuts lacks resources, and must behave as policeman for a generation of surly anarchists who don't receive any discipline at home. These parents don't attend PTA meetings so that they might understand what teachers and schools are up against in a time of greed, or what the stock market calls excessive consumption, when the country club set in Washington is willing to sacrifice the younger generation as long as they're getting theirs; but ultimately, there is no excuse for literate parents not helping with the tutoring of their children.

And if parents can't read or write, there are programs available to them that will help.

The Second Start Adult Literacy Program is one. According to information compiled by this program, thousands of California adults are unable to write a check, use a map, read a want ad, study election materials, read a ballot, read a lease or other contracts, fill out a job application, or health-insurance form, read street signs or warnings on cleaning supplies.

On September 5, my ten-year-old daughter Tennessee and I joined members, tutors and students of the Second Start Adult Literacy Program in their celebration of International Literacy Day, at the Oakland Museum. Second Start's literacy campaign involves volunteers who meet with students for two or three hours a week. This effort, part of a statewide program sponsored by public libraries to promote literacy, instructed 3,000 adult students in 1986. Although the names of the students are confidential during the program, Robin Collins, without embarrassment, read haltingly from a written statement, which was remarkable considering the fact that he'd been a member of the program for three months. Brenda Harper, a tutor, talked of how she joined the program and had become so skillful in the use of English that she became a tutor. Both Collins and Harper, pride in their voices, made us in the audience proud.

State Senator Nicholas Petris spoke of his immigrant relatives and of their respect for language and literature. They were keepers of the oral tradition who, in the days before "Leave It to Beaver," could entertain themselves by storytelling. I was reminded of Mike Gold's comment that his father could tell a story that sometimes took as long as two weeks of installments to tell. Italian, Afro, and Irish Americans of that generation had the same ability.

After I spoke, Tennessee, who was born with a learning disability so severe that experts predicted that she would never learn how to read, read from her first book of poems, *A Circus in the Sky*, and as she read I wondered where she would be without her tutors, a devoted mother, and a house in which books are as necessary as food and water.

Pink Moon Park

A story about what happened
When a little girl could not get out of the universe.
There were so many holes surrounding her in the universe
It was like a cyclone's eye she said.

She went into the cyclone
Into the eye of it.
And then she could not see anything
Until she found on the other side of the black hole
Another universe.

It was without black holes
And it was called Pink Moon Park.
It was a pink universe.
Everything was pink.
The trees were pink
The grass was pink
The bubbles were pink
And the people were pink.

She ran across it until she came across
A manhole cover in the sidewalk.
And she climbed out.
And found herself
On Massachusetts Avenue
Near Russell Street.
And Anne the school bus driver
Was still waiting for her.

—Tennessee Reed
From Circus in the Sky
©1987, Tennessee Reed

Three million Californians can't read or write, yet some of our clownish politicians advocate cuts in the library budget. The same people who want to cut back on these programs are crazy about missiles and armaments, and send the National Guard to suppress change in other countries. Maybe if more people could read and write instead of using inarticulate ways to settle their differences, we wouldn't have the need for weapons.

The tutors and students in the literacy programs are doing their part. The parents and the people who design our curricula have to do theirs.

During the research for my novel *Flight to Canada*, I discovered that after the Civil War, thousands of slaves, regardless of age, rushed to free schools where they were tutored to read and write. Through their effort, the illiteracy rate among the ex-slaves was drastically reduced during the years after the Civil War. For them, learning how to read and write was tantamount to emancipation. No one can deny that the selfish eighties, these years that are meaner than a junkyard dog, have taken their toll on millions of people, and that the vindictive budget cuts have caused millions of others, black, brown, yellow, red, and white, to go under altogether, sending them to soup lines and to homelessness, but if you think of the horrors of slavery, and what those ex-slaves had to go through, before and after the Civil War, you have to conclude that few of us have experienced the hardships that they experienced; therefore, if they can do it, and if people like Tennessee Reed can do it, then so can all of us.

And for those misled children who keep us up half the night with their squealing around the corners on bald tires and indulging in other silly expressions of manhood, and who think that literature is silly, I have a story to recount. Last year, an editor from *Playboy* called to ask about a passage from a Christmas novel I wrote titled *The Terrible Twos*. She said they were running an interview with an athlete and he'd quoted from it. His name: Kareem Abdul-Jabbar.

America's Color Bind: The Modeling of Minorities

*E*thnic life in the United States has become a sort of contest like baseball in which the blacks are always the Chicago Cubs.

Not only the commercial but nonprofit media as well—the latter no doubt prodded by right-wing media watchdogs—have discovered that there are bucks to be made and audiences to be attracted by portraying what they refer to as Black America as a social basket case.

On a local station, recently, a "study" was reported that purported to show how much time the children of different groups devoted to homework. The blacks lost, the Hispanics came in third and the whites, second. Asian Americans came in first. The study's methodology wasn't described. Television was never big on brains, and its destiny is probably that of providing twenty-four-hour programming about services and consumer goods available to cocooning yuppies. One expects more, however, from a distinguished columnist like Pete Hamill.

For Hamill, writing in the August 11, 1987, issue of the *Village Voice*, the typical welfare recipient is a lazy good-for-nothing dope-smoking black person, who speaks as if he were a minor character in Disney's *Song of the South* and spends all of his time hanging out at welfare hotels. He also accepts the neoconservative argument that the primary cause of poverty in this country is promiscuous black women. This, of course, is a myth according to those who've actually studied the situation. A congressional report issued in 1986 by the Joint Committee on the Economy blamed high unemployment and falling wages, not the rise of single-parent households, for the seven million increase in the number of poor Americans since 1979.

Elizabeth Drew recently reported that while the number of out-of-wedlock white children has increased, black illegitimacy is on the decline; also, the largest incidence of out-of-wedlock births occurs in Nevada, a state with a small black population. Other studies show that there is as much rural as urban illegitimacy, a word that has become another code name for blacks.

In response to some of Hamill's other observations about welfare, Barbara Ehrenreich and Frances Fox Piven, authors of *The Mean Season: The Attack on Social Welfare*, cited a General Accounting Office review of over a hundred studies and an extensive survey of its own. The review and survey concluded that welfare does not encourage family breakup or childbearing among unmarried women and that it has little discernible effect on the incentive to work. In their reply to Hamill, published in the *Voice* on September 8, they also noted that "children born into families on welfare are no more likely to end up on welfare than are other children from poor backgrounds."

The most glaring omission in Hamill's article was the fact that two-thirds of the people on welfare are white. They are, in the words of Harvard's Mary Jo Bane, testifying before a congressional committee, "the invisible poor," those who live in middle-class or mixed-income neighborhoods. I'm sure that there are thousands of Irish Americans among those "whites" who've lost their jobs for the same reason as many blacks, the decline of the agricultural economy and the loss of manufacturing jobs, as well as the exportation of unskilled jobs to overseas markets, but I doubt if Pete Hamill would write that these white ethnics are lazy and don't want to work. The only politicians I hear discussing "the invisible poor," the millions of white ethnics on welfare, outside of Jesse Jackson, are representatives of the American ultraright.

Hamill ended his uninformed and folkloric comments about welfare with a recommendation that blacks emulate Asian refugees: The Model Minority.

Ironically, blacks and Hispanics were not always the unmodel minorities, a term that could come to mean resistance to Anglo values. ("Being Chinese is like having a club foot," Ben Tong, San Francisco State faculty member and noted psychologist, quotes an assimilated Chinese American as saying.) In the eighteenth century, blacks were considered the "model minority" by slavers who considered them to be better workers than Native Americans and European indentured servants. Since that time, immigrant groups have been given a succession of "model minorities" to emulate. In the early part of this century, for example, Italian Americans were encouraged to fashion their values after those held by Irish Americans.

About ten years ago, what the press refers to as "Hispanics" were held up to blacks as the model minority, but apparently, due to the large numbers entering the United States, re-Latinizing California, which at one time belonged to Spain and Mexico, it has been decided that Hispanics may pose as many problems as blacks, who, like Latinos, have been regentrified out of urban areas like Berkeley and New York, where, under the Koch administration, the city undertook a program of Puerto Rican removal.

Newsweek, in one of those lazy cliche pieces on Black America, even consulted a Japanese American professor and an Asian American reporter to comment upon the rift between black men and black women, a rift which, according to critic Mary Helen Washington, is media inspired. So not only are Asian Americans the model minority, but they are enlisted as the scouts who tell the settlers what the heathens are up to.

(As a "paranoid" black male, I sometimes feel that people like Ron Takaki, the *Newsweek* consultant, and Yale's Harold Bloom latch onto the skirts of the right-wing black feminist movement so as to avoid the criticisms of feminists from their own backgrounds.) While Professor Takaki is worrying about black feminists getting a man, he seems to be ignoring the conflict between Japanese American men and women over the issue of "marrying out." Nationally, between sixty and seventy percent of Japanese Americans are marrying whites. "They are abandoning the race, giving up on a people they feel has no history, identity, culture or art," Frank Chin wrote in the Asian American magazine *Tea Leaves*.

Misogyny is an issue among Chinese-American male and female intellectuals. Genny Lim, critically acclaimed playwright and author of *Paper Angels*, traces the misogyny in Chinese American communities to China. It was imported to the United States and complicated by factors such as racism and the fact that, unlike in China, the roles of men and women in America became confused. This confusion has caused the breakdown of the Chinese American family, a theme that recurs in Lim's plays. She also pointed to "marrying out" as an issue, not only among Chinese and Japanese Americans, but Korean Americans as well.

Asian American men, for their part, echo accusations made by black males that women are more successful in a white patriarchal society than men, who are considered a threat. "You don't see a yellow anchorman sitting next to Wendy Tokuda," is a complaint I've heard many times from Asian American males.

Other tensions in Asian American communities are caused by poverty, crime, abuse of the elderly (200 cases in San Francisco's Chinatown within the last two years, according to the Chinatown-based Self Help for the Elderly) and bigamy, which resulted from the exclusion laws prohibiting men from bringing women to the United States, so that in some Chinese American families a man has an American wife and an overseas wife.

Every time I hear people like Glen Loury and Thomas Sowell talk about how prosperous Asian Americans are, I'm tempted to ask the elderly Vietnamese women I see rummaging through garbage cans around Lake Merritt whether they drove to the site in a Honda. Genny Lim talks of poverty among Korean and Philippine Americans as well as among Southeast Asian refugees who, in her words, are at the bottom of the totem pole, while the media concentrate on American-born suburban Chinese Americans who, though college-educated, cannot aspire to the same jobs as whites. Southeast Asians are covered by the media when a refugee child becomes class valedictorian, Ben Tong adds. He says that there are not even middle-management positions available for the educated model minorities, because they're not considered to have leadership or executive qualities. Tong cites a definitive study compiled by Amado Cabezas, associate professor of Asian American studies at Berkeley, on the disadvantaged employment status of Asian and Pacific Americans. The study, which became the basis for Cabezas' testimony before the 1980 Civil Rights Commission, claimed that though the educational attainment of Asian Americans exceeds that of whites, their income level is not that much higher than that of blacks and Hispanics.

Tong traces the model minority phrase to a speech given by Hubert Humphrey at a Chinese American high school, during which Humphrey praised the Chinese Americans for not rioting and for demonstrating, in Tong's words, how a properly colonized people are supposed to behave.

Tong says that being a model minority means that a few folks are allowed to jump through the hoops and make careers of being good servants to the white power structure. Genny Lim sees the model minority phenomenon as part of an attempt to divide Americans of Asian origin from other groups.

In keeping with the American pattern of assimilation, crime is also becoming a problem in Asian American communities. When I heard of an Asian gangland shoot-out in Seattle, I called my friend, novelist Shawn Wong, to congratulate Chinese Americans for becoming All-American at last. Asian American gangs are involved in extortion, prostitution and drugs throughout the United States. According to the *San Francisco Chronicle*, November 3, 1987, overseas Asian "triads" are forging alliances with California gangs. Those gangs include the Wo Group, 14K, Chiu China, Luen Group, Tung Group, United, Bamboo Gang, Four Seas, Niu-Phu Gang and others. The Asian Gang Task Force reported to Congress last year that both Asian American criminals and businessmen in New York and San Francisco are making hundreds of millions of dollars from heroin and investing it in real estate in both cities. A front-page article in the *New York Times* reported that the "Chinese Now Dominate New York Heroin Trade" and that they are distributing heroin to dealers in the city's poor neighborhoods.

Ben Tong offered a possible explanation for the growth of youth gangs, who, like Oakland's youthful black drug dealers, are so bold that they defy the ancient ethnic associations and patterns. Frank Chin, writing in *Quilt* magazine, says, "The one rule of Chinatown warfare . . . is: Don't endanger white tourists. Don't shoot up valuable restaurants. The boys who jumped into the Golden Dragon restaurant in San Francisco in 1977 and shot up the place . . . declared war on all of Chinatown with their boldness."

Similarly, black hoods who came of age in the forties and fifties express shock and outrage that skinheaded black punks would assault the elderly, something unheard of in their day. (According to wiretaps conducted on the phones of powerful members of organized crime, a young Italian American hood was almost wasted for referring to a don as Fat Tony to his face.)

Tong says that the possible explanation for the rise of the Asian American youth gangs is peer group pressure. Inner-city Asian kids have it rough, he said. "Most of them have to work, their families are poor, they have no mastery of English, they attend crowded schools, and some of the Asian kids don't make it and are summarily disowned by their families."

Just as there exists black-on-black crime, and before that Irish-on-Irish crime and Italian-on-Italian crime, yellows are becoming victims of yellow-on-yellow crime. Under the head "Asian Crime Victims Ending Silence," the *New York Times* ran a story about Vietnamese immigrants who have settled in

Philadelphia over the past decade and become victims of robbery and extortion by Vietnamese youth.

The problems that exist in Asian American communities have been ignored by the hundreds of op-ed columns, editorials and endless articles in model minority-boosting magazines like *Newsweek* and *Time*. These magazines that are so concerned about Asian Americans never review books by Asian Americans, unless they are tokens. Since the sixties there has been a renaissance among Asian American writers, yet few are known to the general public, and publishers won't publish them because they're considered too ethnic.

If yuppies and Georgetown neoconservatives admire Asian Americans so much, how do they explain the often brutal treatment that Asian Americans receive in this country? After reading a *New York Times* reporter's comment that a black man was killed in Howard Beach because of black underclass behavior, I wrote a letter asking the *Times* why Asian Americans were being assaulted all over the country, when they are considered to be model citizens. (It wasn't printed.) When I arrived in Boston last February, I heard on the radio that although the assaults on blacks had declined in Boston, assaults on Asians had increased. According to an *Oakland Tribune* editorial, "Anti-Asian sentiments—expressed in violent attacks, racial slurs and political activities—have occurred across the land, even in the 'tolerant' Bay Area. The motives for the anti-Asian backlash vary widely, from economic competition to fear, ignorance and racism."

Asian Americans are in a tragic situation in which they are used by people like Pete Hamill and abused by working-class whites like the ones who murdered Vincent Chin, a Chinese

American, because they mistakenly thought that he was Japanese, and later were acquitted.

Asian Americans are also being assaulted on university campuses, a situation that makes the position of those die-hard Western civilization fanatics even more deplorable. Their opposition to an ethnic studies requirement is similar to the position that George Wallace took when he stood in the schoolhouse door, as a way of turning back change. They're so intellectually dishonest they don't inform their students that if it were not for African scholars and writers, there would be no Western civilization, or that West African and Native American cultures have had as profound an influence upon our hemispheric civilization as the European. They are probably ignorant of these facts. Moreover, we don't have to get along with Plato, but we certainly have to coexist with citizens from backgrounds different from ours, and it's about time we learned something from their cultures. For my money, those who oppose the multicultural curricula are just as guilty of fomenting hate and racism in American society as the Klan and the Nazi Party, probably more so because their influence is wider.

Most Asian Americans I've talked to agree with Genny Lim and Ben Tong that the model minority image being promoted by the neoconservatives and the media arises from cynical, corrupt and devious motives, or, as Shawn Wong quipped, "White racist love is just as insidious as white racist hate." They also agree that to depict Asian America as a fantasy land where everybody gets A plus and adheres to the work ethic as though millions of blacks don't—blacks who helped to build the Southern agricultural economy, the industrial North and the cattle-herding West—is just as dehumanizing as referring to black America as a place where people hang out in front of welfare hotels and shoot up. As Patrick Chew, assistant principal of San Francisco's Galileo High School put it: "For every [Asian American] success story, there are ninety-nine failures." Every group has its Joe Boys and its angels, and just as I'm aware of an Asian American underclass, and a white ethnic underclass neglected by politicians, I'm also aware of yellow and white ethnic scholars, musicians, playwrights, composers, artists, scientists, engineers, theologians, heroes and heroines, gods and goddesses.

Another article by Hamill, an Irish American, which just about led a parade for Bernhard Goetz, a man whose taped confessions could have been authored by William Burroughs, coincided with the police roundup of the last members of an ancient Irish American underclass gang called the Westies. The activities of the four hoodlums who asked Bernhard Goetz for five dollars were mild in comparison to the pastimes of the Westies, referred to as the "Irish Mafia." The Westies have committed thirty murders in the last fifteen years. Michael Cherkasky, the head of the rackets bureau of the Manhattan district attorney's office, said of the Westies, "This is the most violent gang we've seen."

As much as I was offended by Hamill's column, I don't think that it could be construed as deliberately committing slander against black Americans but was based on his fear of seventeen-year-old, 175-pound black "predators," the word Hamill used. I have problems with punks, too, but on the basis of one percent of the black population I wouldn't generalize about the majority, just as I wouldn't stigmatize all Italian Americans as members of the Mafia based on the two-tenths of one percent of Italian Americans who are engaged in organized crime.

I also think that the article reflects Hamill's career crisis. All one has to do is compare those calm, serene articles that he wrote for the *Examiner* with those *Voice* columns, which read like parodies of the irate letter-writer that Steve Allen used to imitate. One of the reasons the United States seems always to be on the verge of an apocalypse is because the media are based in New York. Some of this bitter fever has rubbed off on Pete. Therefore, I propose that Pete Hamill be given a permanent writer-in-residency in San Francisco, and that he use time in that lovely and classy city to write novels. Pete, California, and American fiction would be the richer for it.

Soyinka Among the Monoculturalists

I distrust the monoculturalists' point of view so much that when they praise something I become suspicious, and when they condemn something, I feel that there must be something praiseworthy about it. This hunch is not always justified, since, from time to time, both they and I agree about the quality of a work, but in the case of Wole Soyinka's play, *Death and the King's Horseman,* I think that the establishment's critics lacked the understanding to appreciate one of the most powerful, and most memorable—possibly unique—experiences I've had in the theater. Their narrow-minded reviews, to put it politely, discouraged many theatergoers from sharing this experience, and for this reason they proved Soyinka's point about the monocultural view of the world and the lack of understanding that goes with it.

Acceptance of African and Afro-American artists depends upon the political fads of the time in this country. Soyinka said as much in the course of an interview with the *New York Times.* Currently, the American intelligentsia (the only difference between the Right and Left of which is the Left's more creative racism), embrace a smugly blind attitude toward "the other," the fashionable metaphor for the Third World. For them, the problems of the Third World are traceable to a lack of "the work ethic," as one columnist put it. According to the current political daydream, the invasion of Africa and its catastrophic consequences never happened, and slaves, who did "slipshod" work, continued to be imported to the Americas, presumably because the slave masters were lonely. The uplift of the Third World will only happen through the graces of "Western civilization," a term that gives some penurious minds an opportunity to hang out with Aristotle.

Therefore some of the publications that bashed Soyinka's play had some kind words to say about V. S. Naipaul's *The Enigma of Arrival*, a book whose racism was soundly rebuffed in a devastating review by Derek Walcott in the April 13, 1987 issue of *The New Republic*. The *Village Voice* critic, who came to the play with an obvious chip on her shoulder searching for evidence of patriarchal oppression (she works for a newspaper owned, directed, and published by men, as Olunde would point out), took Mr. Soyinka to task for his "tribalism," yet Mr. Naipaul's book was listed in the *Voice* as "our kind of best-seller." Mr. Naipaul told the newspaper *India West* (25 April 1980) that Negroes were "the most stupid, primitive, lazy, dishonest, and violently aggressive people in the world." As for the charge of "patriarchal" oppression in *Death and the King's Horseman*, Iyaloja, "Mother of the Market," is the strongest character in the play. She scolds the king's horseman, Elesin Oba, and defies Simon Pilkings's order prohibiting Iyaloja from stepping across a line during her stockade interview with Oba. In scene 3, schoolgirls ridicule and humiliate the muslim patriarch, Sergeant Amusa.

Perhaps some of the critics were offended by the portrayal of Simon Pilkings, the district officer, and his wife Jane, because, according to the current political line that has trickled down from Washington and taints American cultural life, they were bringing the values of a superior culture to "savages." They accused Soyinka of "comic-strip" and "agitprop" creations with the Pilkingses, even though in scene 5 Pilkings gets in some good lines during an exchange with Elesin, whose death the Yoruban religion requires for the sake of cultural continuity. For her part Jane, who offends the local religion by joining her husband in wearing a confiscated juju costume to a ball, shows sensitivity to other aspects of the culture, so much so that her husband chides her for being a "social anthropologist"; a comic-book character would be incapable of the kind of intelligent dialogue that she conducts with Olunde, Elesin's son, in scene 4.

It's a good guess that some critics and members of the audience, who identified with the Pilkingses, are descendants of people who suffered under colonialism as much as the play's Nigerians, but took the Pilkingses' side because, in the United States, the fastest route to "whiteness" is to identify with the "Upstairs" of "Upstairs, Downstairs" and other imports that American television borrows from the BBC. This is the reason that the British royal family receives more coverage per year than all of the black-ruled nations of Africa.

Moreover Americans, both black and white, have always had trouble understanding African religion. African religion, for example, has always been ridiculed, misunderstood, and suppressed in this hemisphere. The reviews of the play show that such attitudes are difficult to change. A religion that claims millions of followers (its key zones being New York and Miami) was referred to as a "cult" by one critic. *The Christian Science*

Monitor dismissed Yoruban religion as being based upon "tribal superstition," Mary Baker Eddy's theories presumably being based upon fact.

Critics have difficulty dealing with a "pagan" religion of such potency that even Amusa, the play's Muslim, respects it and Olunde, the "been to," and "not quite," remains a follower. Responses to this religion by bigots have often produced disasterous results. During the famous Witchcraft Hysteria, when some of Salem, Massachusetts's young women were possessed by some of the same gods mentioned in Soyinka's play, many of the citizens were executed. Tituba, the slave who was held responsible for the young women's trance, was imported from Barbados, where a variation of African religion known as obeah is practiced. She was jailed.

Mr. Soyinka reports that some of the members of the Vivian Beaumont audience, as well as members of the cast, became "overwhelmed" during the performances of the play as the powerful *gbedu* drum did its work. As Pilkings observes in scene 2 of the play: "It's different, Jane. I don't think I've heard this particular sound before. Something unsettling about it." This is not your ordinary theater, and it's quite possible that the term "play" doesn't begin to encompass what Mr. Soyinka achieves in *Death and the King's Horseman*. His theater has more in common with the ancient religious possession dramas of the Greeks that included gods that were parallel to those of the African ones—human gods with human appetites, who, unlike Jehovah, could accept ridicule from mortals.

The Greek connection is appropriate since, rather than polarizing cultures, Mr. Soyinka gently draws parallels between them. While in some societies the king's horseman is required to accompany the king to the otherworld, it is the custom in others for captains to go down with their ships. Costuming and dancing are universal. Soyinka is not the first to explain European tribal wars and World Wars I and II as instances of mass suicide; Carl Jung and poet Wilfred Owen have said as much. So that empires don't tilt, some societies require that their royalty take risks, such as making dangerous trips to their far-flung outposts. Writer Robert Maynard has even suggested that President Kennedy's trip in a convertible through a hostile Dallas was an act of hubris.

Mr. Soyinka is a cultural relativist who uses different literary and dramatic traditions in order to create a theatrical synthesis. In the play both Yoruban and English are spoken by the actors, while the music of different cultures, including indigenous dances, the waltz and the tango—a dance of love and death that arose from the slums of Argentina—are performed.

Speaking to me in one of the Vivian Beaumont offices, shortly after the play's production on Sunday, April 22, Mr. Soyinka was quite upset, to put it mildly, about the critical reaction. He believes that the "irrational" misunderstanding displayed in some of the reviews reflects a larger problem. A problem of perception that many of the nation's outsiders, including Ralph Ellison and Richard Wright, have reflected upon in their masterworks, *Invisible Man* and *Native Son*, a book in which blindness is a frequent image and metaphor. The sort of cognitive dysfunction, or plain arrogance, that would lead a president to send a Bible as a goodwill gesture to a people whose sacred book is the Koran.

After another discussion with Wole Soyinka of the critics' reactions to *Death and the King's Horseman*, the following Friday morning, by coincidence, I had an engagement at Bob Fox's class at the University of Suffolk on Beacon Hill in

Boston. Professor Fox, a Polish American who grew up in Buffalo, New York, is one of a growing number of young Euro-American writers, scholars, and critics who don't treat African religion in the usual Tarzanized manner. One thinks of Robert Gover, author of *Voodoo Contra*, and Bob Thompson at Yale, whose work on African religion has led to his ostracism by some of his colleagues; the campus issue of *Newsweek* ridiculed one of his courses on the subject. *Newsweek* is the same magazine that sighed relief when Lisa Bonet, star of *Angel Heart*, the standard exercise in Hollywood "voodoo," promised that she wouldn't be doing any more voodoo dances. (The term "voodoo" has come to denote Americanized African religion; some speculate that it is based upon the word "vodu," used by the Fon people to refer to the orishas, loas, or "spirits" of their Yoruban neighbors.)

I asked Bob Fox, a friend of Soyinka's in Nigeria, for his reaction to some of the critics' comments about the religious aspects of *Death and the King's Horseman*. He said: "For anyone to term African traditional beliefs 'tribal superstition' demonstrates vividly that Eurocentric arrogance and ignorance are alive and still kicking. Whatever stands outside our monological enterprise troubles us, and if we can't control or influence it, we put a pejorative label on it. But this demeaning terminology can be turned back on us. After all, the linkage between apartheid and fundamentalist theology in South Africa reveals a racist system built on Afrikaner tribal superstition. And I think this is a clue to what lies behind some of these radically misinformed statements about Soyinka's work. My impression is that there are people who want to put him 'in his place' because instead of ingratiating himself with his 'masters,' he had the nerve to use the occasion of his Nobel Prize to attack Western hegemony in general and apartheid in particular. But then Soyinka has always refused to be 'Westoxicated,' and the richness of his Yoruba cultural heritage has enabled this resistance."

Before climbing Beacon Hill to Bob's office, I paused in front of the statue of Mary Dyer. A Quaker, she was hanged in the 1600s for her membership in an unconventional faith. As I examined her proud stone face, staring out at me from underneath a bonnet, I thought of Pilkings's line in *Death and the King's Horseman:* "You think you've stamped it all out but it's always lurking under the surface somewhere."

An Evening in
Radcliffe Yard

*T*he sideburns on his partially balding head gave him a distinguished look, like a photo of a Fisk graduating class member taken in the nineteenth century. He was wearing a light blue shirt with white collars, a yellow tie with black dots, a dark blue Brooks Brothers suit, and black cordovans. As I sat listening to David Evans, I heard him recite the familiar magazine and newspaper op-ed themes; in fact, he'd written some of the same material in a *Newsweek* column. He spoke of how the black middle class is alienated from "the underclass," and of the career and consumer goals of the present generation of black youth. His ideal graduate would be one who was steeped in black history and tradition and committed to the "community service," values that are stressed by black colleges but ignored in white colleges, or reluctantly added to the curriculum.

Evans would like black graduates to follow his example. He is the son of an Arkansas sharecropper, whose father and mother died when he was a boy. His oldest sister dropped out of college in order to support her brothers and sisters. He received a BA from Tennessee State and a degree in Engineering from Princeton in 1966, but these tickets to the middle class didn't lead him to abandon what he would call his "less fortunate brothers and sisters." While working on the Apollo and Saturn programs in Huntsville, Alabama, he tutored the children of blue-collar workers in the Edmonton Heights neighborhood. He was able to gain admission to college for over one hundred of these children from 1966 to 1970 and since then has presided over the graduation of hundreds more from Harvard and Radcliffe colleges.

On June 10, the Wednesday before my Friday conversation with Evans, which took place at Byerly Hall, a vine-covered brick building near Radcliffe Yard, I addressed the black members of the Radcliffe-Harvard class of 1987.

I told Judith Jackson, a graduate who'd invited me to speak, that rather than indulge in the kind of pontificating one associates with this kind of task, I'd read some poetry and songs scheduled to be set to music by American composers for an album entitled *Conjure II*. I almost didn't make it.

That morning, a nurse at the Harvard walk-in clinic had recorded my temperature at 100.8 degrees. The first doctor she asked to see me refused. "Ishmael Reed," the doctor said when she saw my name. "I despise him. He's very controversial, you know." I had never met the woman and figured her to be a *Village Voice* reader. After a conference with her superiors, the doctor was allowed to go to lunch, and my case was handed over to a black doctor. I was glad to see him, after listening to the other doctor's outrage at the mention of my name. I couldn't help thinking of my grandfather, who was allowed to bleed to death after entering a Chattanooga hospital in the 1930s. "Let that nigger die," the nurse said, according to family legend.

When I arrived at Radcliffe Yard, the ceremony was in progress. It was held under a yellow-and-white striped tent.

The mood was sombre, and the handsomely attired families were waiting for their childrens' names to be called. Some had traveled by car from as far away as Oklahoma and Tennessee, stopping off to see friends on the way.

When I rose to speak, after a generous introduction by Ms. Jackson, I attempted to lend some levity to the occasion by remarking that as a visiting professor at Harvard, I was required to obtain a 100-degree temperature and during the last week await a cab for over an hour. Later I'd read that David Brinkley attended a party with a 104-degree temperature because he didn't want to disappoint his hosts. Maybe each generation becomes softer. That's what I was hearing as I watched scenes from another commencement address on television scolding the class of 1987 for its materialism.

I told the audience that maybe the older generation didn't want the class of '87 to screw up this utopia they've created and invited everybody to join me for a swim in Boston Harbor, an example of the older generation's concern for ecology. (The city itself was being overrun by rats.) I said that I didn't have any advice to mete out, because at forty-nine I still hadn't figured the whole question out. I read some poems and songs about love, about comedy, about death, and about being haunted. I read a poem about an earthquake that had no conscience because it had never attended theology school. I finally read a tribute to the planet Earth in a poem that argued that without this planet, we'd have nothing to stand on.

I was given polite applause, and upon returning to my seat, I noticed that I was feeling better. The Cambridge breeze was cooling me off. But maybe there was another reason for my improved mood. The scene of these young people in celebration, having survived many of the gauntlets that lie in wait for them in a society often cruel to them and their aims. If there was such a thing as August Wilson's "life-force" in Afro-American people, this new race, conceived in North America, neither African nor European, possessed it. It was this life-force that the old spiritual must have had in mind in the refrain, "I ain't gon' let nobody turn me around." It was this force that inspired a man standing in the rear of the Albany College chapel in Albany, Georgia, where I attended a memorial for Dr. Martin Luther King, Jr. in January. The week before, the Klan had shown its behind in Forsyth County, Georgia, and when it seemed that the younger people had forgotten the verses of "We Shall Overcome," he shouted, "We are not afraid."

Though I had intended to leave the ceremony immediately after my presentation, I remained for another hour or so. At the conclusion of the graduation, I posed for pictures with the students and their proud families. It was then that it occurred to me that nobody from the press was there to cover this event. Where was the author of the book about Edmund Perry, an Exeter student, who was killed while allegedly mugging a policeman, as if to show that "educating" a person of his background was futile? Some of the students graduating in the Harvard-Radcliffe class of '87 were from similar backgrounds. Why were there no syndicated features or books about them? Where was the user-friendly black writer who told the *New York Times Magazine* (which seems more and more to be edited by Irving Kristol) that there were no talented black faculty or students, only to be corrected by scholar Diane Pinderhughes in a follow-up letter? He had no reply. Where was *Newsweek*, which devotes more time to the "black underclass," one percent of the Afro-American population, than to the remaining ninety-nine percent, and which, during the week of the class of '87's triumph, carried stories about a black man murdering a white woman, and a black man using the AIDs virus as "a weapon," a page apart?

You really can't blame the commercial media for not being present, because they don't pretend to have any class. But what about National Public Radio, which during the week of June 10 repeatedly ran a story about how black kids couldn't succeed in the academic world without being accused of "going white" by their peers? Blacks wouldn't have survived if they hadn't become familiar with the symbols of the "white world," which seems to prove that they're more cosmopolitan than some of their fellow citizens who advocate a military solution for dealing with cultures different from theirs. How many of their fellow citizens can place Nicaragua on the map, as well as the other demonic zones that politicians teach them to despise? And how about their intellectuals, many of whom still refer to Europe as a continent? National Public Radio is always reminding us of the low scores by blacks on "IQ" tests.

Where was the PBS, which ran a documentary concocted no doubt by the feminist ideologues who've captured New York's channel 13, blaming the famine in Africa on sexism? If you think that's weird, in 1986 they produced another documentary during which even the producers, who made money from her songs, blamed Billie Holiday's problems on black men. PBS in Boston also produced a slanderous documentary entitled "Street Cop," in which black Roxbury residents were depicted as crack dealers and bums. The station was so high and mighty that it didn't feel obligated to respond to the letters of protest it received.

They weren't there, but I was. That's what I meant when

I told Tray Ellis, a young writer, that a black writer, in order to survive, has to be versatile. And so I took off my commencement speaker's mask and assumed that of a stringer journalist recording the event for posterity.

For over thirty years I have been a poet, novelist, essayist, and songwriter. Thomas Hearns would understand. He is a man who knows his way around the welterweight, middleweight, as well as light heavyweight divisions. Writin' is Fightin'.

Ishmael Reed grew up in working class neighborhoods in Buffalo, New York. He attended Buffalo public schools and the University of Buffalo. As well as being a novelist, poet, and essayist, he is a songwriter, television producer, publisher, magazine editor, playwright, and founder of the Before Columbus Foundation and There City Cinema, both of which are located in Northern California. Among his honors, fellowships and prizes is the Lewis H. Michaux Literary Prize, awarded to him in 1978 by the Studio Museum in Harlem. He has taught at Harvard, Yale, and Dartmouth, and for twenty years has been a lecturer at the University of California at Berkeley. He resides in one of Oakland, California's black pogroms.